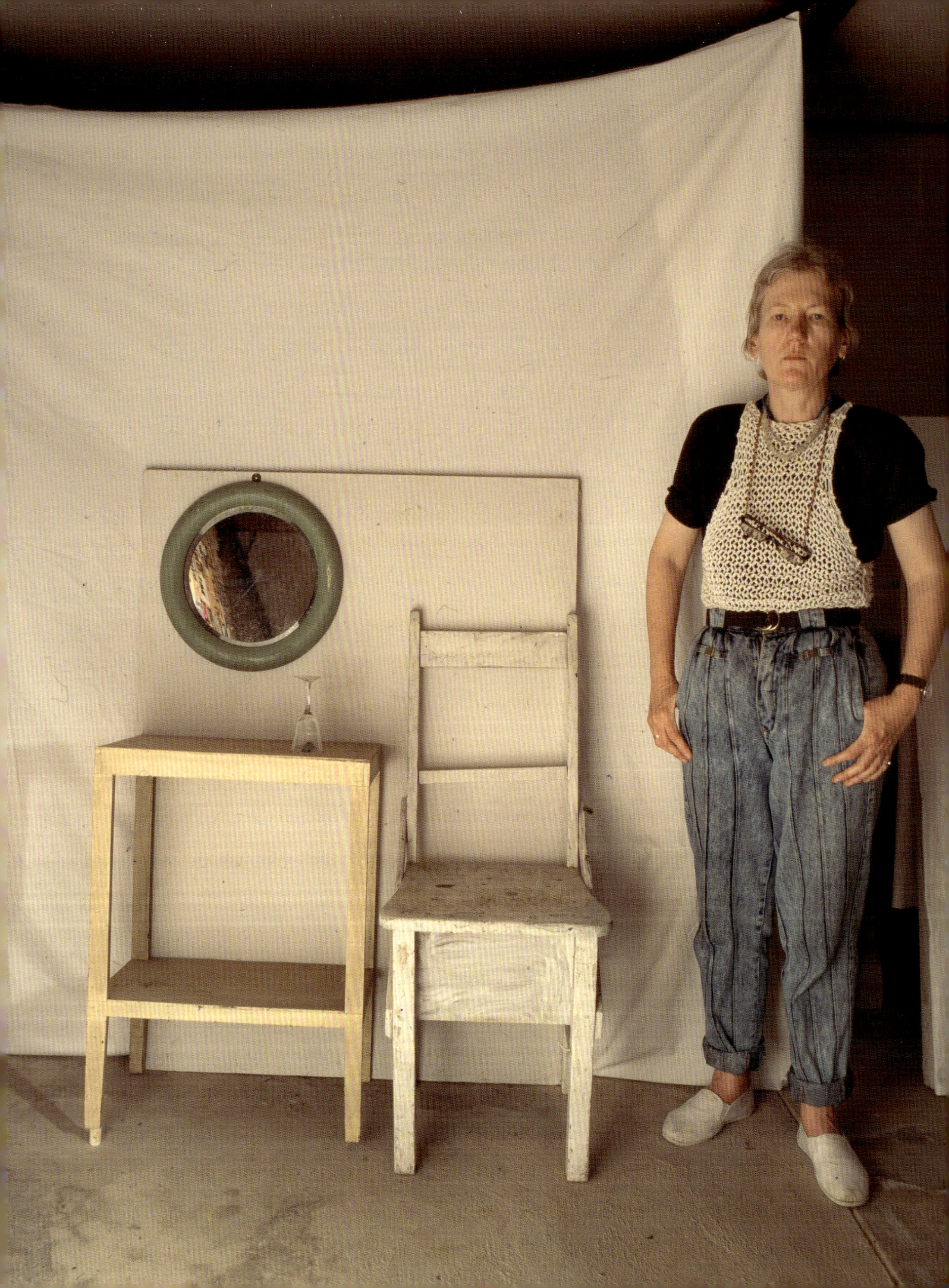

MADONNA STAUNTON
OUT OF A CLEAR BLUE SKY

QUEENSLAND ART GALLERY | GALLERY OF MODERN ART

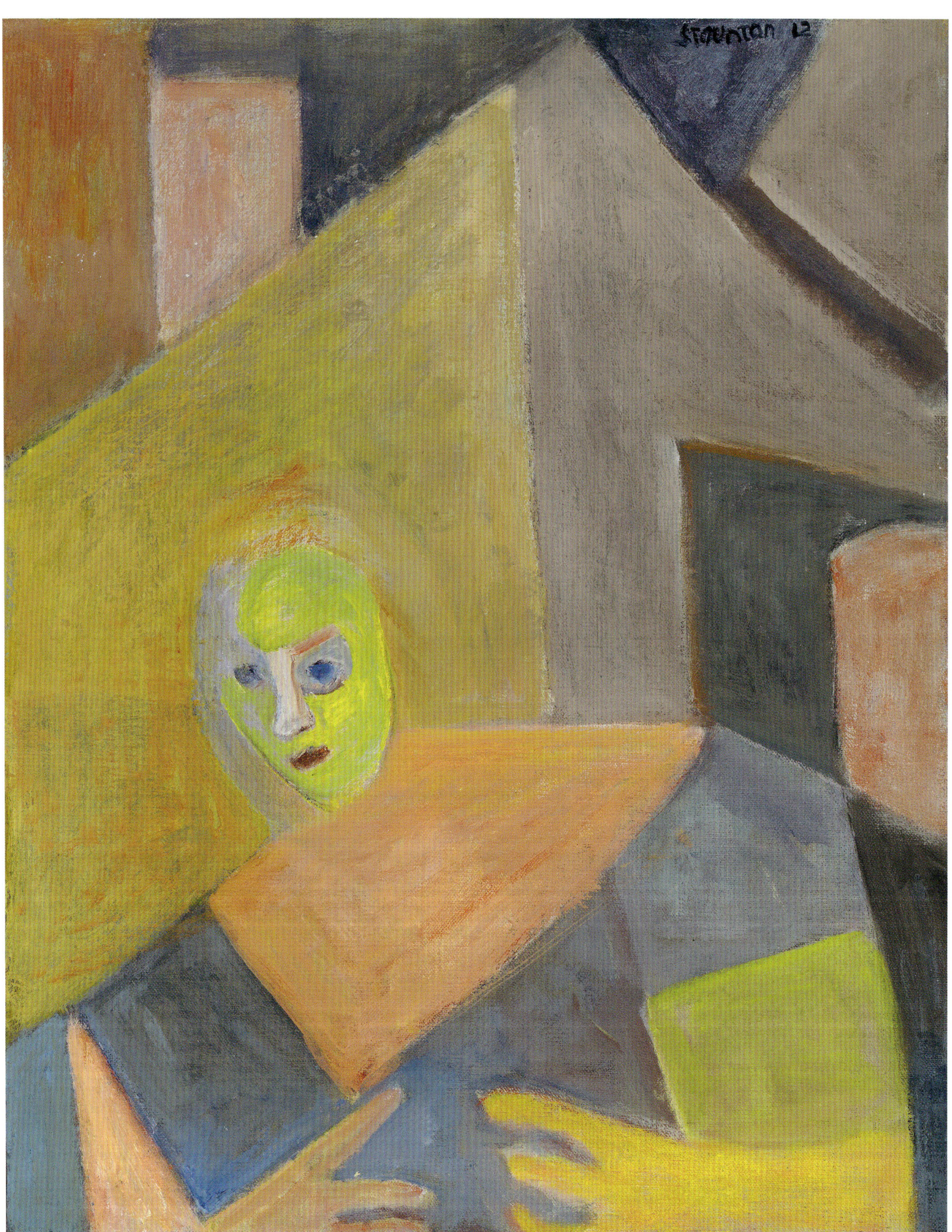
STAUNTON 62

CONTENTS

Anxiety (detail) 2012
Synthetic polymer paint on canvas board
51 x 40.7cm; 56.2 x 45.8 x 4.3cm (framed)
Purchased 2014 with funds from the
Estate of Jessica Ellis through the
Queensland Art Gallery | Gallery of
Modern Art Foundation
Collection: Queensland Art Gallery

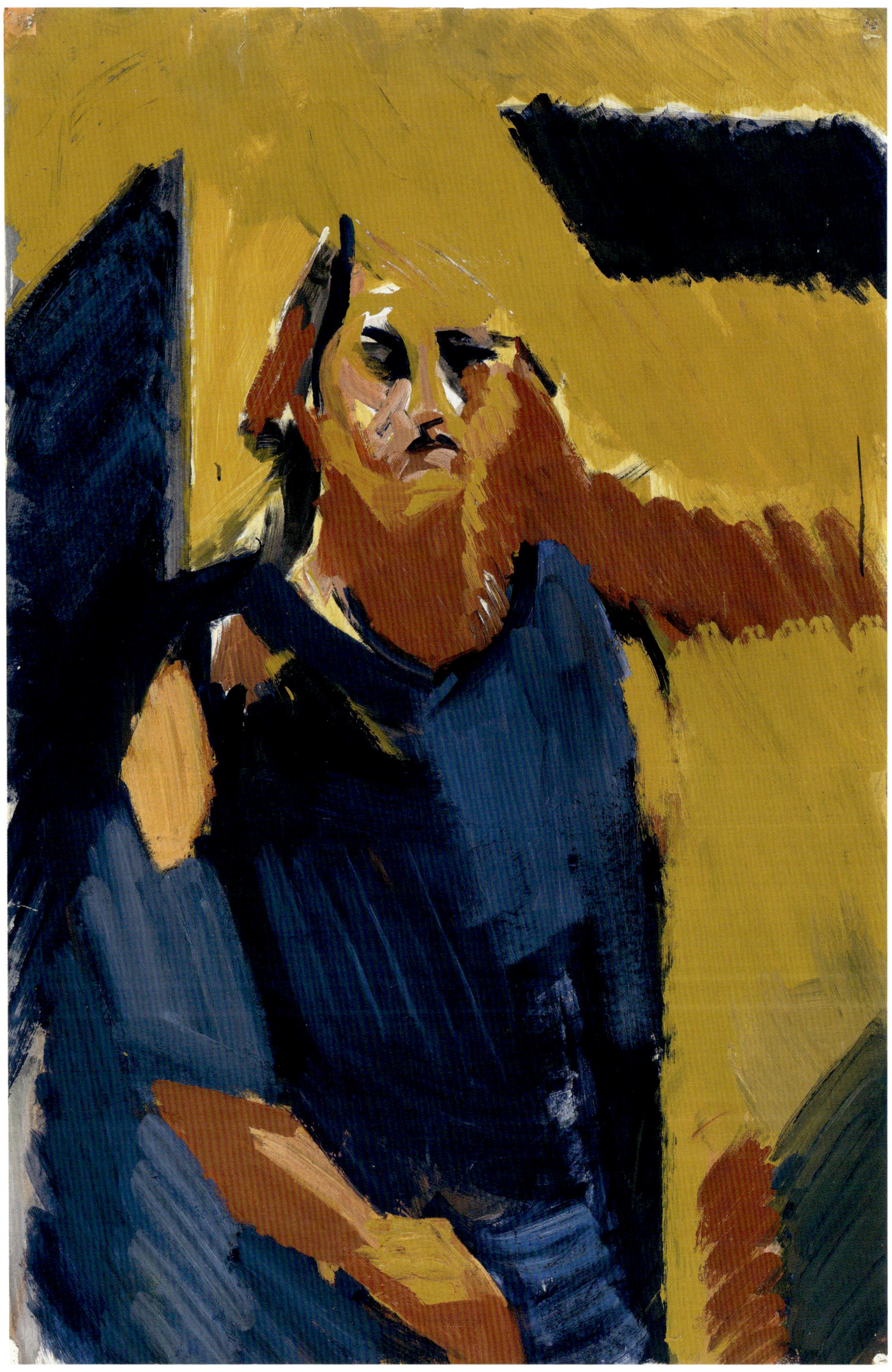

THE GLENCORE QUEENSLAND ARTISTS' GALLERY PROGRAM

Glencore is proud to be one of the Queensland Art Gallery | Gallery of Modern Art's leading corporate sponsors, with a partnership dating back to 2006. Our support of the Gallery's Emerging Indigenous Art Award series, then as Xstrata Coal Queensland, raised the profile of emerging Indigenous Australian artists and assisted the Gallery in strengthening its collection of contemporary Indigenous Australian art. Following the success of the three-year award program, QAGOMA established the Queensland Artists' Gallery program and an associated regional touring program with our support.

This partnership has profiled the work of some of the most recognisable and influential Queensland artists working across painting, photography, drawing, sculpture, textiles, pottery and design. These have included LJ Harvey, James Fardoulys, Vida Lahey, Lloyd Rees, Daphne Mayo, Carl and Phillip McConnell, Ian Fairweather, Ruth Stoneley, Richard Stringer and Sam Fullbrook. At the same time, touring workshops have offered residents of regional Queensland hands-on opportunities to work with leading practitioners in fields including quilting, clay and photography. The Queensland Artists' Gallery program has also included three Artist's Choice exhibitions, in which leading Queensland artists are given free reign to curate a display from the QAGOMA Collection. To date, artists Lawrence Daws, Marian Drew and Michael Zavros have participated.

Glencore, which merged with Xstrata in 2013, is one of the world's largest global diversified natural resource companies. We are proud of our contributions to the Queensland economy, and consider the creation of opportunities for Queenslanders to engage with the art of the state to be a crucial aspect of our corporate social investment.

We are very pleased to continue this support with 'Madonna Staunton: Out of a Clear Blue Sky', an important late-career survey of one of Queensland's most vital and continuously evolving artists.

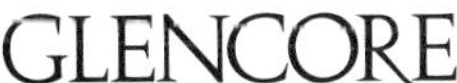

Woman in motion c.1995
Synthetic polymer paint
112.2 x 75cm
Collection: The artist

FOREWORD

Chris Saines, CNZM

The Queensland Art Gallery | Gallery of Modern Art (QAGOMA) is very pleased to present this timely, and in many ways surprising, exhibition from one of Queensland's most significant practising artists, Madonna Staunton.

During her teenage years in the 1950s, as she was steering toward an as-yet undefined career in the arts, Staunton explored writings on philosophy and theology, among them *The Perennial Philosophy*, Aldous Huxley's deft curation of the commonalities between Eastern and Western mysticism. Huxley delved into methods by which the seers and sages attained a 'more than merely human kind and amount of knowledge':

> It is only by making physical experiments that we can discover the intimate nature of matter and its potentialities. And it is only by making psychological and moral experiments that we can discover the intimate nature of the mind and its potentialities.

We could read this as symbolic of Staunton's practice. Over four decades her experiments out of the lineage of Dada, Constructivism, Fluxus and Abstract Expressionism have been touchstones of Australian modernism. Working from a basis of Formalism, she infuses her work with a deeply personal streak that has grown stronger as her practice has matured. Indeed, her physical experiments have crossed a boundary to reveal the intimate nature of the mind.

'Out of a Clear Blue Sky' tallies the tension of this duality, as emotion materialises from Formalism. It expands our understanding of Staunton's work, often considered to be most grounded in collage and assemblage, to position painting at the centre.

The exhibition highlights this confident return to her passion for painting. Following early abstract works of the 1960s, health issues put large-scale paintings beyond her reach. Here, we explore the techniques Staunton subsequently used to paint without painting — collage and then assemblage — in the face of this challenge.

Whatever the medium, the composition, tonality and harmony of her work have always suggested a painterly essence, while an appreciation of textures and tactile experiences, drawn from her mother's and grandmother's history of craftwork, imbued her three-dimensional work with a striking physicality.

'Out of a Clear Blue Sky', named for one of a large number of new works, acknowledges the cloaked emotions of a great Queensland artist. From painting to collage to assemblage to painting, it also celebrates a full circle. Twenty years since her last major survey at QAG, organised by the Queensland University of Technology, and more than ten since her solo exhibition at Brisbane's Institute of Modern Art, we are grateful and honoured to be able to present this exhibition and include within it such a prominent body of new work.

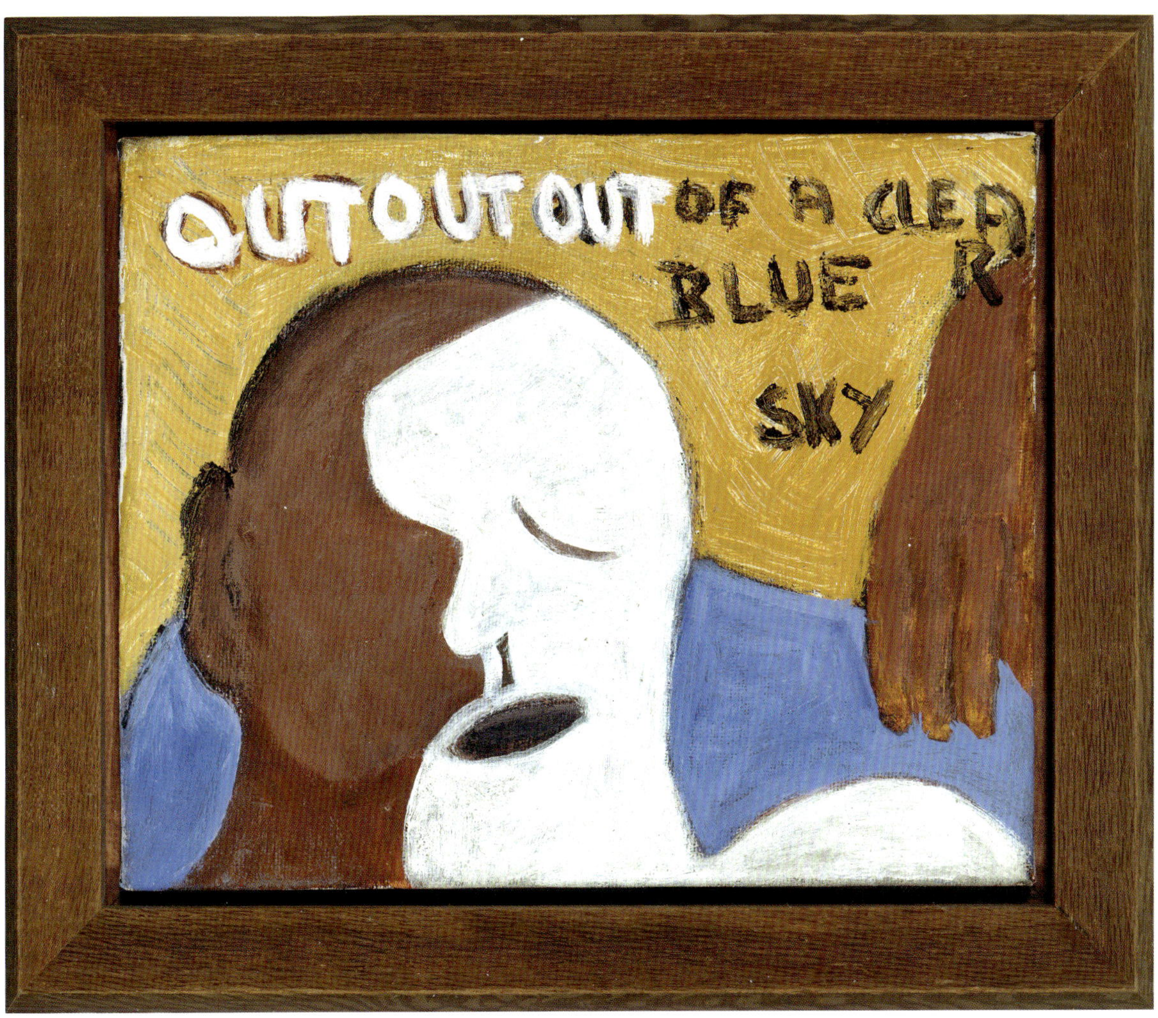

I must warmly congratulate Peter McKay, Curator, Contemporary Australian Art, QAGOMA, on both the exhibition and the publication. Peter has brought a great deal of sensitivity and visual intelligence to this task. I also thank Glencore for their ongoing support of the Queensland Artists' Gallery program, without which we could not undertake the vital research and exhibition of the work of Queensland artists in projects such as this.

I particularly wish to thank Josh Milani of Milani Gallery who has facilitated the loan of almost half the works in the exhibition from a raft of very generous private collectors. I acknowledge the many institutions and collectors who have loaned works: Queensland University of Technology; Griffith University; University of Queensland Art Museum; Grahame Galleries + Editions and several others.

Finally, and most importantly, I want to sincerely thank Madonna Staunton for her openness and her resolve to push her practice forward throughout an astoundingly rich career.

Out of a clear blue sky 2013
Synthetic polymer paint on canvas
20 x 25cm; 27.3 x 32.5 x 4.4cm (framed)
Purchased 2014. Queensland Art Gallery | Gallery of Modern Art Foundation
Collection: Queensland Art Gallery

'Out of a Clear Blue Sky' represents a sense of aching hope that comes from an appreciation of life in all its great complexity, capturing Madonna's instinct for expression and her remarkable sense of self. It is an exhibition that we are proud to present.

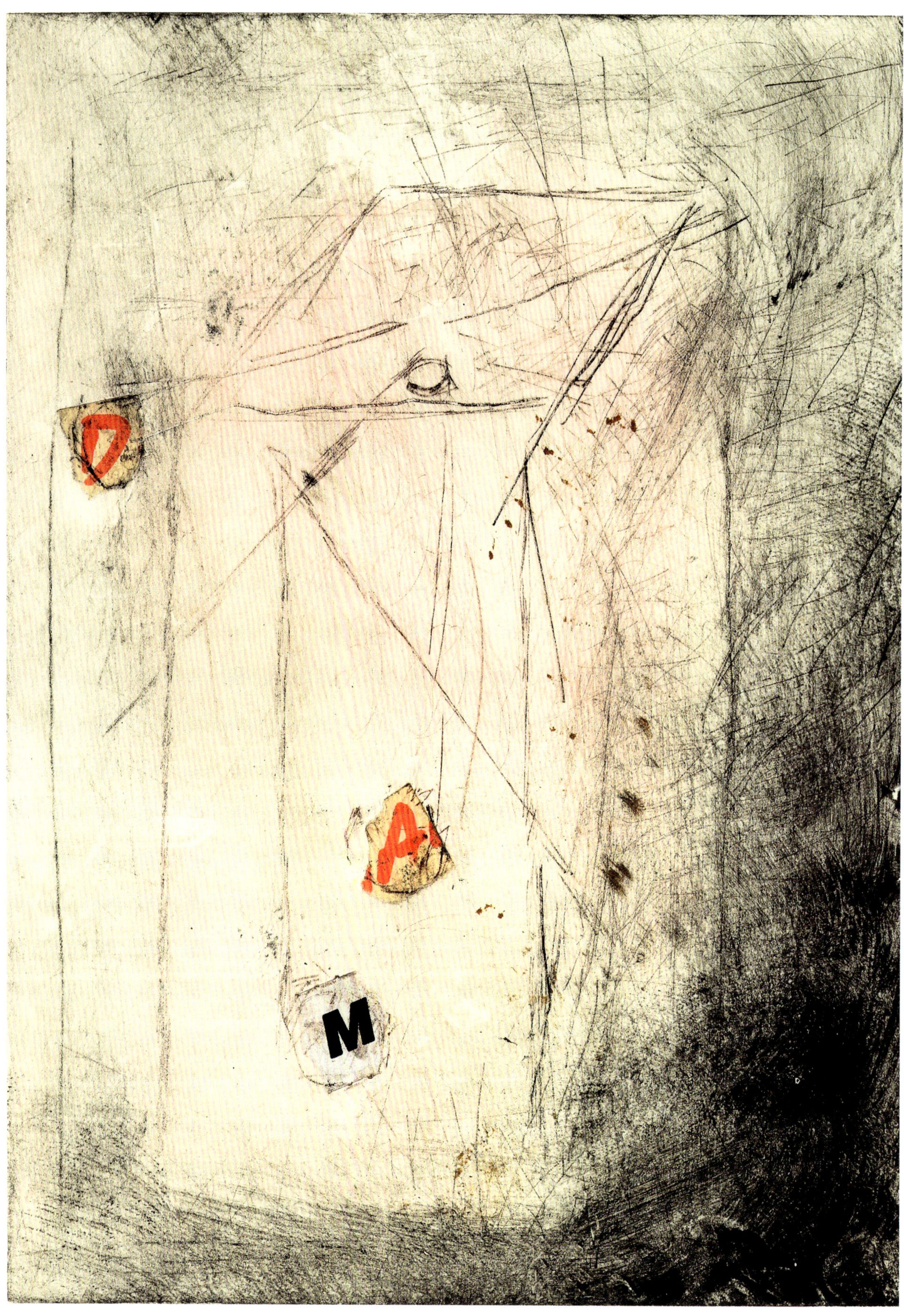
D
A
M

HIDING IN FORMALISM[1]

Peter McKay

'Perhaps all I've lost
Might be looking for me'

(Madonna Staunton)

Renowned for being an artist of restrained elegance and abstract harmonies, Madonna Staunton would presently be better recognised for her unswerving staging of authentic emotions and vivid philosophical insights. In her recent practice she has taken to piercing through the everyday with an erudite brush. Personalised, yet commonly relatable, Staunton portrays her learning from an inventory of life events and broad observations in graphic accuracy.

Staunton is an adventurous artist who has worked across many media, but her abundant talents in collage and assemblage have undoubtedly overshadowed her more recent venture into painting and print. Within the many stories of Australian art, Madonna Staunton can be considered the most proficient practitioner to have worked in collage, and one of the most significant figures in assemblage too. Her talent for harmonising colour, tone, shape and texture is rarely equalled and the allusive potential she brings forth from the most modest materials is testament to the 'common' miracle of the world and all its elements. Yet this achievement has greeted her with some limitations, as she should also be noted as an important contemporary painter — one who delves deep into the psyche to disclose her insights into mortality, morality and the experience of our interior worlds.

Having edged towards prominence since the late 1960s, Staunton has often been positioned as a regional modernist given her attachment to the creative current of the time. She has sometimes been respected for, though to some degree relegated to, being a quiet campaigner for the advancement of European and American aesthetic values in Australia. While this discussion adequately places Staunton in the wider schema of art history, on occasions this focus on concept or technique and associated narratives has arguably unfairly diverted the discussion from the inimitable particulars of her own practice.

Around 1999, Staunton started on a long return to figurative painting. She began to leave this conflation with art history behind, and focused intently on articulating her personal vision of life and human nature. Subject content that she might have previously buried in Formalism was now out in the open, and soon the artist was making paintings that would measure among some of the most powerful and provoking works of her career. In plain sight, Staunton reinvented and, given the thoughtful philosophical content, possibly even rediscovered herself.

These disjunctions have necessitated a solid reappraisal of the art of Madonna Staunton. Here we reconsider her lifetime of achievements from this vantage of her most recent figurative paintings, not simply to balance the history, but to also consider the idea that Staunton has always been a painter. Painting is certainly where her practice began and, on careful viewing,

Untitled suite (Closet) (detail) c.2001
Etching, collage
3 sheets: 17 x 13cm (each)
Collection: The artist

it is possible to see that in many ways she never stopped being a painter. Staunton simply stopped painting with paint and instead painted with found materials, ready prepared in colour, tone, patternation, texture, and even form, by their experience in the world at large.

Furthermore, Staunton has also created a substantial body of print work in etching, solvent transfer, collotype and, most significantly, in monotype. This is important because the monotype method is in essence a variation on painting, except that the image is first composed in ink on a smooth plate before being pressed onto paper. The swiftness and self-assurance required to compose a monotype means that the process lends itself best to those artists that can improvise, be spontaneous and embrace the fortuitous accident. These are characteristics that Staunton has spent a lifetime cultivating — or has at least been preserving from her youth.

Beginnings

Whereas every artist's life experience has some impact on the shape and content of their creativity, in Staunton's case this influence offers valuable insight into the structure and content of her work, which often harbours a biographical aspect. Her father was a bookshop owner and collector of period furniture, and her mother was a librarian and book conservator, poet and painter, who studied under the educator, advocate and utopian intellectual William Lane. She was born 6 October 1938 in Murwillumbah on the New South Wales Tweed River, 130 kilometres south of Brisbane, the only child of Albert Errol Staunton (1905–62) and (Violet) Madge Staunton née Jones (1917–86). The family moved to Sydney the next year, and the young Staunton attended a number of Catholic schools until 1951 when, at the age of 13, they relocated to Brisbane. Owing to ill-health, Staunton did not return to formal schooling, however, she continued to study, and later teach, music privately. Living in a household full of books and bibliophiles, she became an avid reader. Soon she started writing poetry with some seriousness.[2]

Although Staunton was raised in a family with high participation in the arts, it seems her father was not always entirely sympathetic to his daughter's aspirations to be an artist of one sort or another. From early childhood Staunton was a talented pianist, yet she still remembers the impact of her father's remarks after stress caused her to falter on stage during a recital. He declared on the journey home that she did not seem to have what it took to be a performer. In her fragile state, the young Staunton's hopes were dashed. This scene may be the subject of the small semi-abstract painting *Allegory* 2012, and in broad thematic terms this relationship dynamic would seem to be implicated in many works. In the cultural context, this parenting style may not have been unusual at the time in Australia, yet its impact persisted.[3]

At 16, Staunton entered the workforce. Although she landed promising entry-level positions in the literary section at the *Courier-Mail* and in Grice's Music Store, in little over a year she was given an invalid pension and left the workforce. Staunton has explained:

> At the age of seventeen I was losing the natural physical energy and exuberance that goes with adolescence. That made me a much more introverted person, someone who was thrown back on to one's own resources . . . I think the book that really set me off on an inner journey . . . was *The Perennial Philosophy*. It opened up a world of mystical literature to me. Any form of fulfilment was to be very much a journey into the wilderness.[4]

Allegory 2012
Synthetic polymer paint on canvas
25.2 x 20.1cm; 31.4 x 26 x 3.8cm (framed)
Collection: The artist

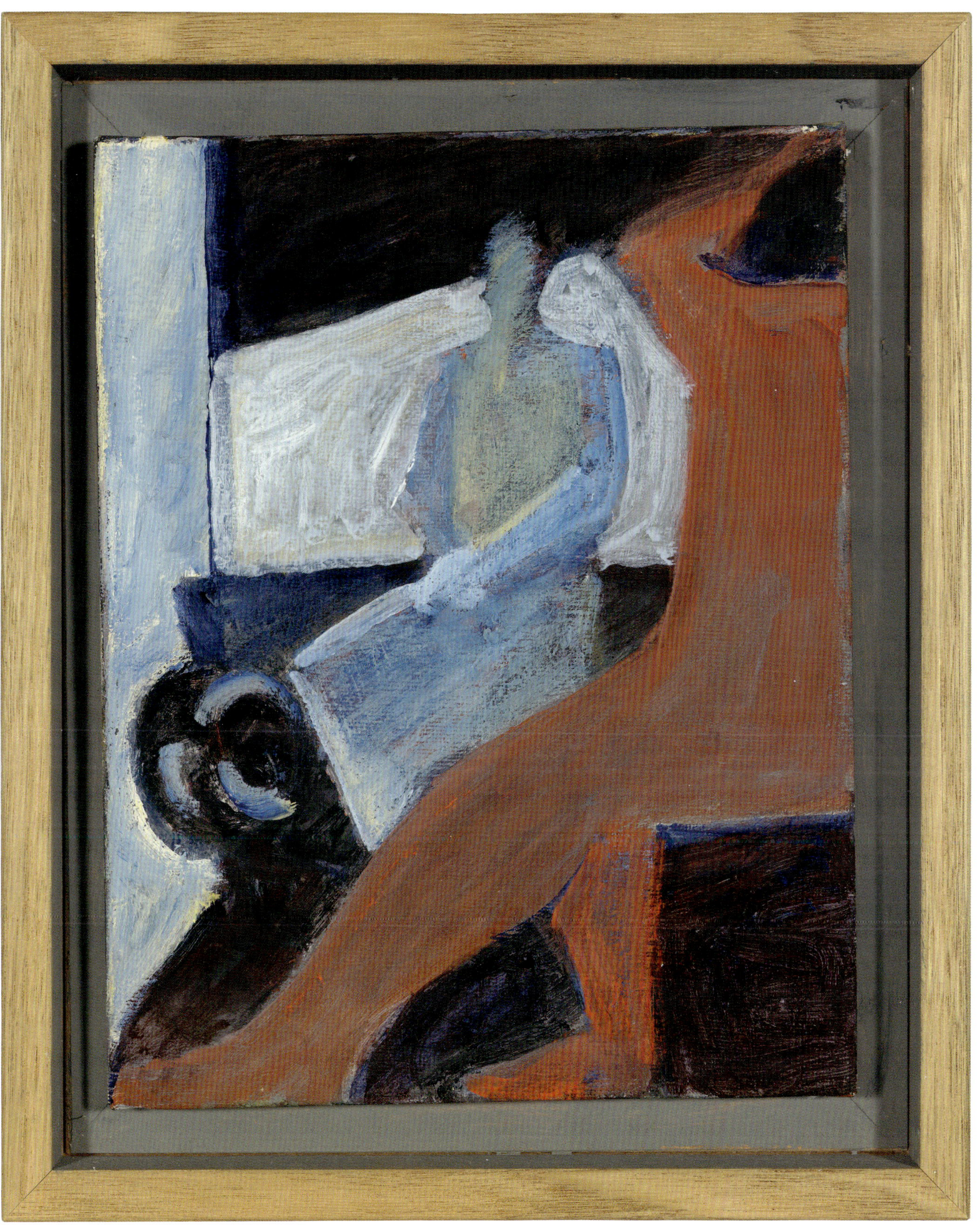

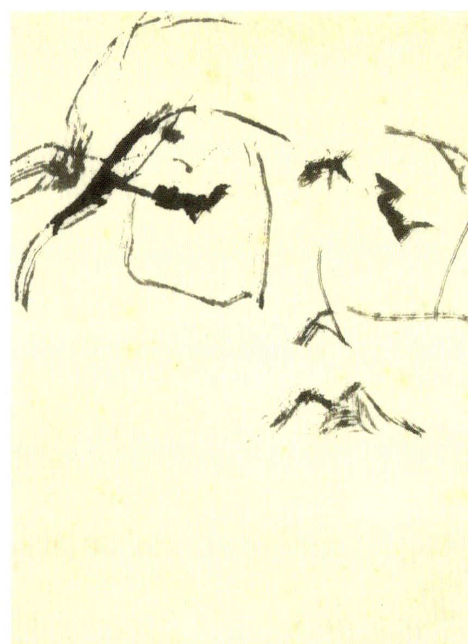

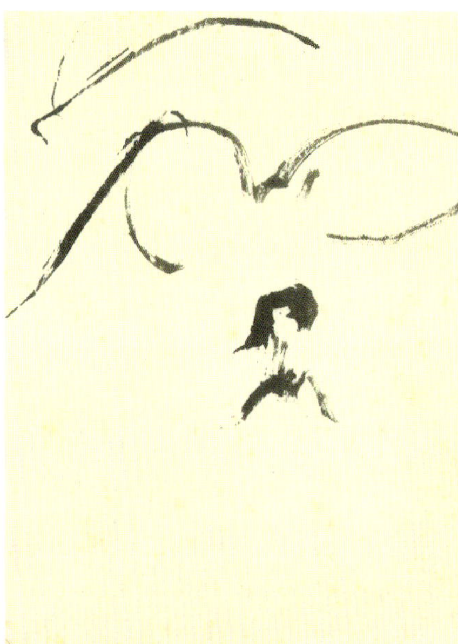

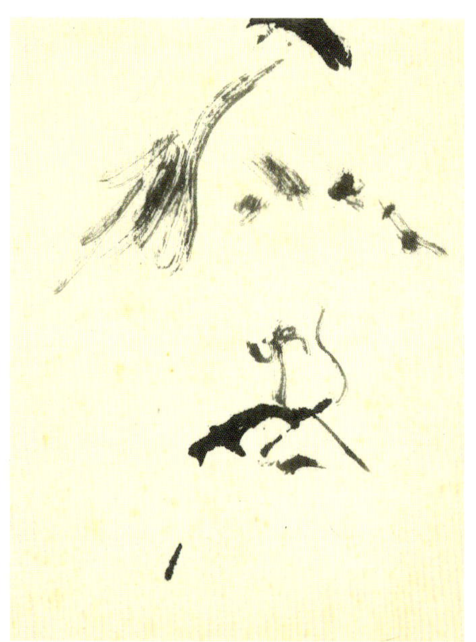

Circumstance brought isolation, but this was not to be a time of loneliness and disenfranchisement as one might expect. Instead, Staunton profited from solitude and reflection. In the manner of Henry David Thoreau and his classic description of the simplest life possible in *Walden; or, a Life in the Woods* (1854), Staunton found that her spirit was strengthened and focused by the absence of distraction and interference. She learnt that a life that gives full attention to its content is more rewarding than a busy life, which often fails to engage beyond the task at hand. Solitude became Staunton's key to transcending her immediate surrounds and striking a dialogue with the universe. This is how the passage to the artist's inner world opened.

Thinking of Aldous Huxley's achievement in *The Perennial Philosophy* (1945), we should appreciate that mainstream views on spirituality, mysticism and the contemplative experience of the mind have changed markedly between then and now. Published shortly after World War Two, Huxley's text demonstrated the shared concepts among many different religions, and in doing so participates in a long tradition of comparative texts looking to articulate the character of the human spirit in its highest form. It should be noted that Staunton is not particularly concerned with religious command or ideologues. *Authority* 2013 — a portrait mocking those (patriarchal figures) with no consideration for the individual and their experiences and who dress in the robes of moral expert — demonstrates her nuanced relationship to concepts of a spiritual nature. Staunton emphasises the expanded dimension of our own inner worlds and the need to recognise the inner worlds of others.

The Perennial Philosophy was also the artist's introduction to Buddhist thought, which would become fundamental to her relationship with material and form. In the catalogue accompanying Staunton's first survey exhibition, Michele Helmrich astutely commented that the artist's work 'pays tribute to the Zen ideal that Enlightenment is to be found in the commonplace, in emptiness or non-attachment, rather than in European preoccupations with emotion or intellect.'[5] It should be emphasised, however, that Staunton is not an aspirant Buddhist — simply that her outlook is aligned with a Buddhist account of the world and associated ideas on how to be in it.

Self portrait c.1980
Ink
31 x 23cm

Self portrait c.1980
Ink
31 x 23cm

Self portrait c.1980
Ink
31 x 23cm

Collection: The artist

Without labouring the point, it is important to understand something of the nature of the Buddhist insight. The following passage from the *Tao Te Ching*, the classical Chinese text that contributed to the foundation of Taoism, Buddhism — and the artist's personal library — deserves a slow reading and contemplation. Quite remarkably, this cryptic play about understanding the fragile and elusive nature of passing time accounts for Staunton's art practice in its several guises, or its processes rather, as well as any passage ever could. Staunton's art is indeed that of keeping track of things; of exerting only a gentle influence, taking care not to force a direction; of cultivating the inherent experiential wealth in each element, irrespective of and above its *material* value.

> What is not moving is easily held. What has not happened is easily planned. What is brittle is easily broken. What is tiny is easily dispersed. Deal with a problem before it arises; exercise control before confusion exists.
>
> A tree with an arm-girth of trunk grows from a tiny sprout; a nine-storied terrace arises from a heap of dirt; a thousand-mile journey begins with the first step. Action spoils; reaching loses. The truly wise are not active. Thus they do not spoil things. Do not reach so do not lose. Things are often spoiled very close to completion. Be as careful at completion as you were at the beginning.
>
> Thus the truly wise want the unwanted and do not prize what is rare. Study what is unstudied and preserve what is lost. Assist in the course of nature but never interfere with it.[6]

Although thoughts and emotions can take a surprising amount of time to form, their presence may be felt long before. One may feel a certain way, or hold a particular belief well before being able to adequately articulate, let alone thoroughly examine, a position. These elusive and influential intellectual objects could be hiding, or they might well be hidden: either way, it takes a sophisticated strategy to catch them and make them something more tangible than intuition. As Staunton's subjects shifted, this approach to discovery and creation has remained constant. It is the art of being present.

Education

The artist's mother Madge had studied painting at East Sydney Technical College from 1948 to 1951; she took great care to relay much of this learning to her daughter and support her independence through education. Notably, Madge studied with prominent artist and designer Phyllis Shillito, who provided her pupils with a sophisticated foundation in colour theory. Madge's exercise books became the foundational knowledge for her daughter — providing Staunton with an advanced understanding of tint, shade, contrast, scales, complements and discords from a very young age. Interested in furthering this education, Staunton exchanged some solitude for professional development, joining the Royal Queensland Art Society at 21. She took painting and life-drawing classes, participated in exhibitions, and worked on the group's newsletter.[7] Staunton proved to be most proficient at working from life. Her line-work in charcoal was elegant and lyrical, and she was also noted for her ability to capture a perceptive likeness in one sitting using oil paint; there is a joyful, bright and sometimes sensuous quality to them. Italian painter and sculptor Amedeo Modigliani was cited as an early interest in this regard. The subtle tonal shifts and evocative distortions that form the hallmarks of Modigliani's approach became strengths that Staunton would deploy equally across her mature output — albeit in a wholly different tenor.

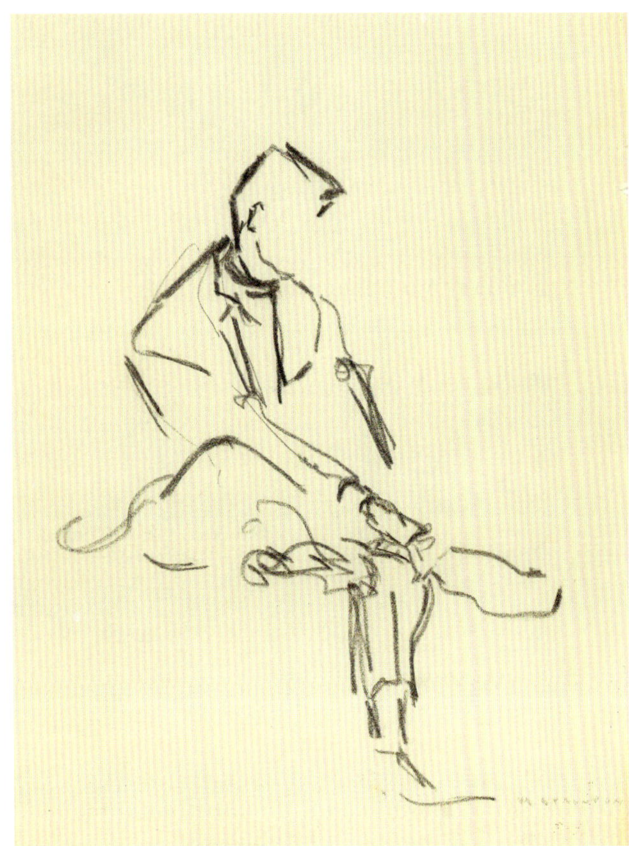

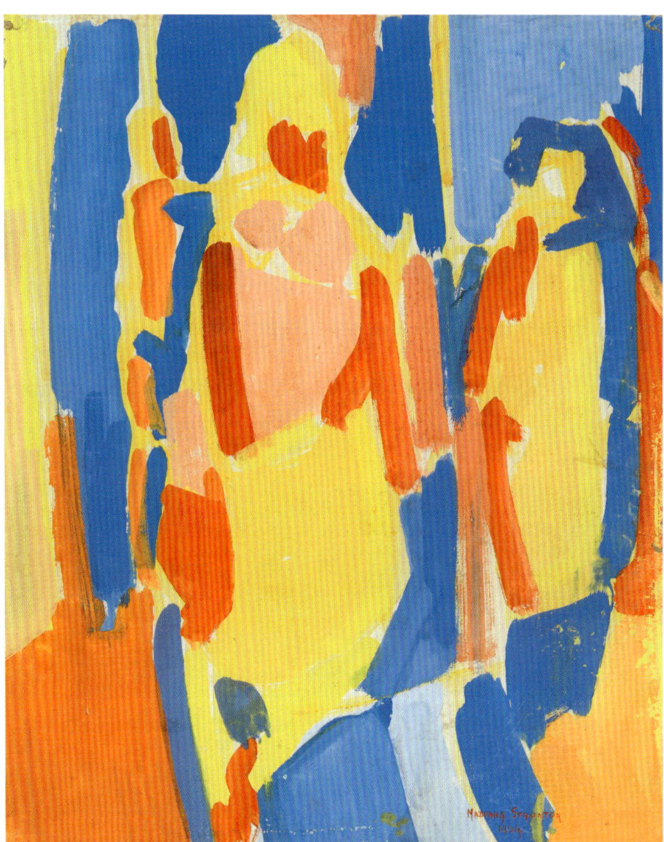

In the excellent introduction to the *Contemporary Art Society in Queensland* by Helen Fridemanis, Staunton explained how this interest became moderated over time.

> At about the age of twenty I looked at the German expressionists. With the re-emergence of Expressionism, I realised that there was chaos within and there was chaos without and the only way I could create order was through art. Being an artist is a tremendous medium for exploring. If you are an artist you are granted that wonderful means of actually giving expression to any discoveries that you have made.[8]

Subsequently, between 1964 and 1965 Staunton attended Brisbane's Central Technical College. Without overstating the significance of a student exercise, it is interesting to note Staunton's capacity to process Roy Churcher's belief in Cézanne and the idea of describing 'form through colour' in only one lesson as is evident in *Pedestrians* 1964.[9] Her mother's support and teaching clearly set Staunton well ahead in this regard. A more ambitious stimulus might be seen in the loose calligraphic twists found in *Easter* 1967 after studying under Bronwyn Yates in 1966. By this time Staunton, at 29, was now starting to prove herself as an artist of independent vision.[10] *Peripheral green, blue* 1968, for instance, in its remarkably delicate tonal harmony and refined composition, is partly the work of a young artist responding to the then relatively recent American breakthroughs — Abstract Expressionism and more specifically Colour Field painting — but, equally, Staunton was also giving form to her own sensations. Tellingly, the slightly earlier, and largest work of the group, *August 1966*, greatly rewards the viewer who devotes time to recognising the subtle complexity of interactions between its elements. It is tempting to suggest that Staunton's keen commitment to modernist art practice was a

Man Crossed c.1967
Charcoal
44 x 33cm

Pedestrians 1964
Synthetic polymer paint on card
50 x 41cm

Collection: The artist

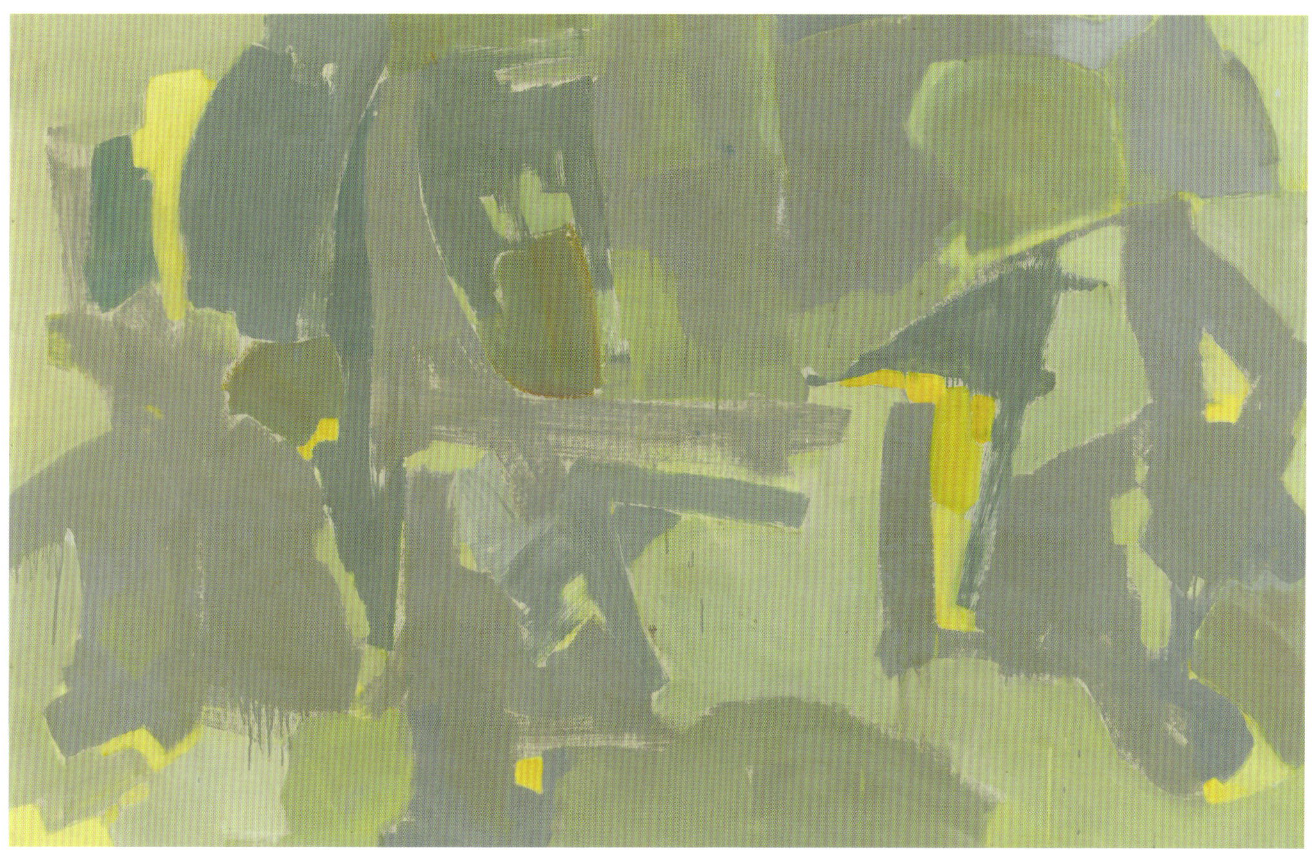

brave and exceptional thing during this conservative era in Queensland's history; and in a broad evaluation, it was. It might also add credence to the regional modernist account too. Throughout its history, however, Brisbane has been host to a more nuanced and multidimensional socio-political setting than it is often ascribed. As Urszula Szulakowska details in the introduction to her history of *Experimental Art in Queensland* 1998, much of the innovation at this time in Queensland was imported, and yet:

> Above all, experimental art in Queensland has often been hybrid in its disregard of formalist divisions between the various arts. Such art challenged Eurocentric ideologies through the artists' working method, which was often collaborative and critical of the market conditions of art production. Directly, or indirectly, experimental artists attacked Queensland's conservative political hegemonies.
>
> In this, they were often articulate, often totally incomprehensible; sometimes caught in a party-time, fashionable poseurship; at other times deeply committed to an impermeable ethical system.[11]

In this context, Staunton's early years exemplify the attitude among experimental artists at the time. This period, rather than laying the foundations for her brand of regional Modernism, is better seen as a period spent recognising her aesthetic interests in the works of other artists, then digesting these ideas and synthesising them into her own style in the process — which is indeed the way of most developing artists.

August 1966
Oil and synthetic polymer paint on composition board
122.5 x 184cm; 124.5 x 186cm (framed)
Collection: The artist

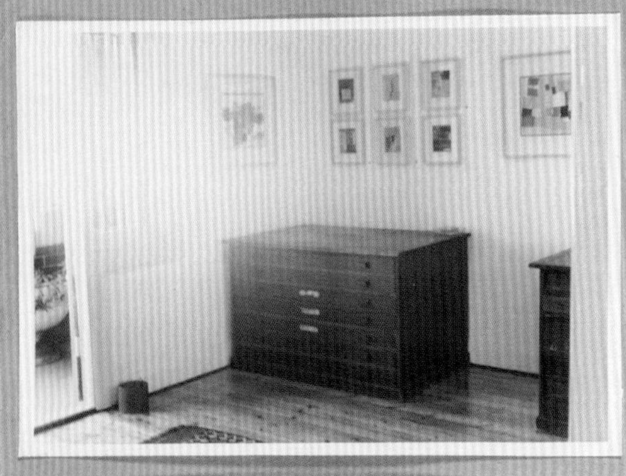

M. STAUNTON — RAY HUGHES GALLERY, RED HILL. BRIS.

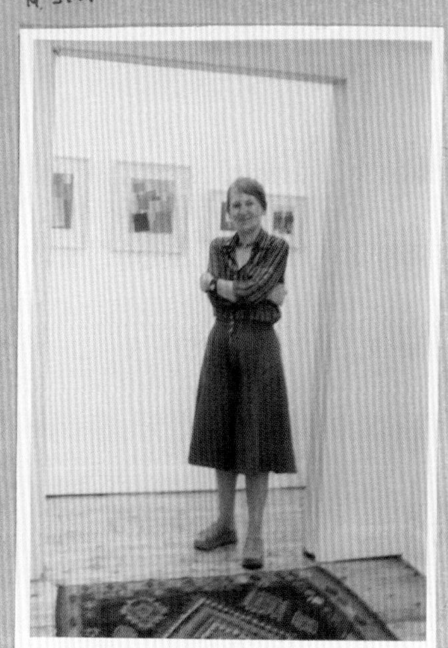

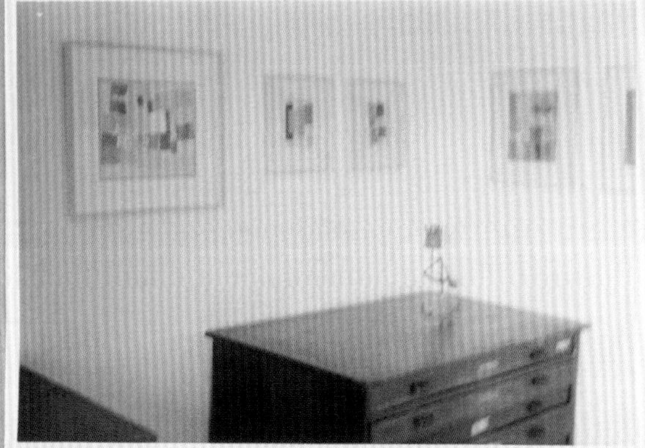

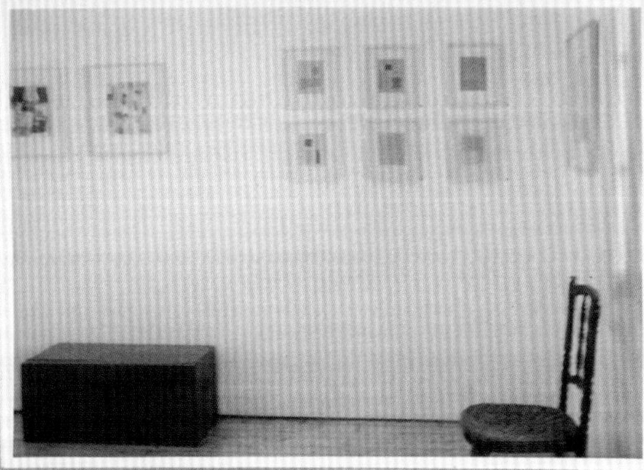

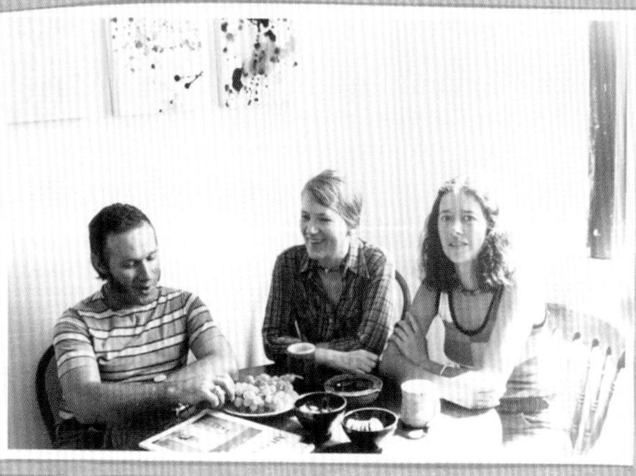

L – R
R MACPHERSON
M. STAUNTON
JILL GODFREY-HUGHES

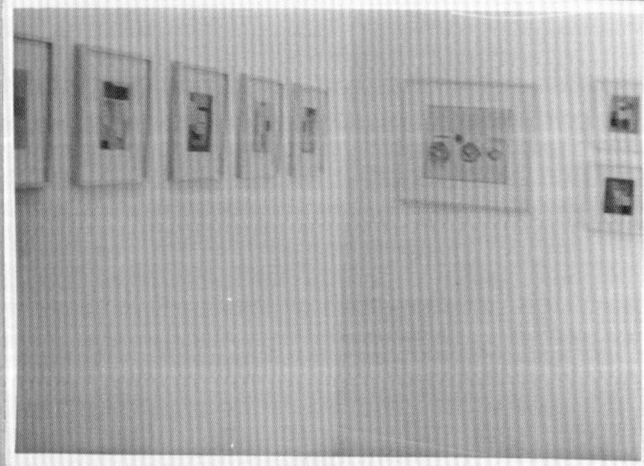

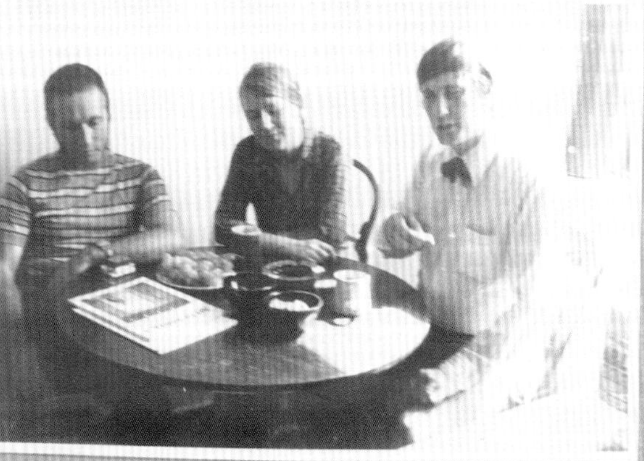

L/BOB MACPHERSON
C/M. STAUNTON
R/RAY HUGHES

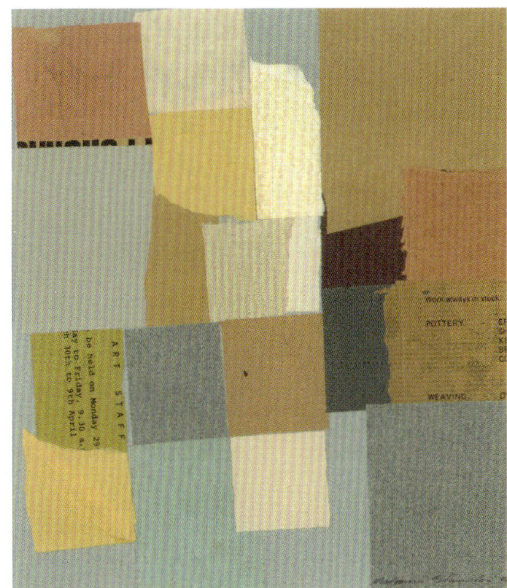
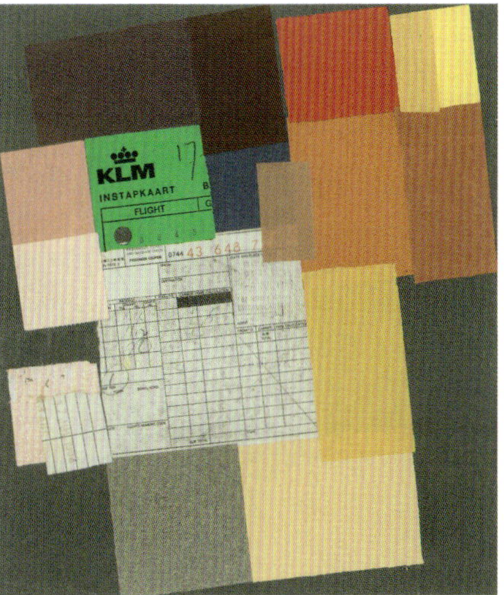

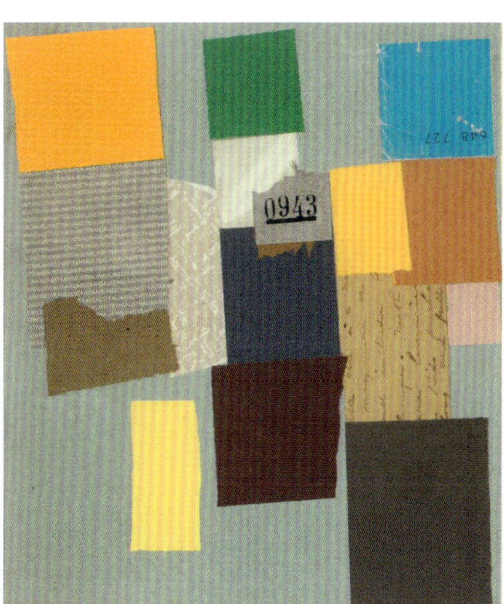

Collage

Staunton joined the executive of the Contemporary Art Society (CAS) in Queensland, serving from 1968 to 1970. This involvement may have proved integral to her fortuitous path toward collage. Her very first collage, made c.1968, was largely composed from CAS newsletters: art about newsletters about art. More truthfully, however, by 1968 her health was sadly failing again, and she no longer felt able to work in paint at a large format. Staunton explained that 'Being an only child, my world became one of textures — a world of tactile, intimate experiences on an intimate scale', and collage seemed to accommodate this awareness.[12] After searching for a method to relay the profound inner world she had been developing with her studies of Eastern and Western philosophy and modern poetry, these limitations imposed by poor health proved oddly fortunate. David Andre explained in the text accompanying the prominent University of Queensland exhibition 'MacPherson, Shepherdson, Staunton' in 1979 that:

> The way in which a flat area of colour is applied to a large surface cannot be duplicated on a small scale — one alternative was collage. While the size of the works was reduced, the monumental scale was preserved. This impression of monumentality is achieved through the restrained use of colour and the avoidance of clutter, an obvious temptation with collage.
>
> To find the muted colours of her paintings, Madonna Staunton looked to those things other people had discarded — faded pieces of cloth, scraps of paper, tags, old photographs, letters, weathered leather and other long-since-forgotten fragments.[13]

By 1976, Staunton was exhibiting collages in a commercial gallery setting with Ray Hughes and at the Institute of Modern Art, which only opened twelve months prior, in the 'painting' exhibition 'Brisbane Painting Today' (1976). The association with Hughes, who was then based in Brisbane, was significant.

> Hughes' promotion of conceptual, minimalist and neo-popist forms in the late sixties and early seventies was crucial in developing an audience for difficult and demanding art forms. The early exhibitions at the Ray Hughes Gallery were of considerable critical worth within Australian late-modernist art, including some of the major Australian women artists. Hughes, to his enormous credit, has always shown the work of many women artists.[14]

Exhibition views of 'Madonna Staunton', Ray Hughes Gallery, Brisbane, 1976
Madonna Staunton archive

Untitled 1976
Paper collage
27.2 x 23.6cm

Untitled 1976
Paper collage
27.4 x 24.1cm

Untitled 1976
Paper collage
27.8 x 24.2cm

The James C Sourris, AM, Collection, Brisbane

Staunton was by this time a significant figure in the rapidly establishing contemporary art scene. This, of course, was also the time that she became known as a collage artist, and much has been written about the influences and connections between her and European modernists such as cubists Pablo Picasso and Georges Braque; surrealists and dadaists Max Ernst, John Heartfield, Hannah Hoch, Jean Arp and Kurt Schwitters; followed by a diverse group of Americans such as Joseph Cornell, abstract expressionist Robert Motherwell, and proto-pop artist Robert Rauchenberg, among many others. While this discussion of chronology and dissemination offers an interesting historical account, it does little to illuminate the understanding of Staunton's practice, as her work is not about or significantly in the style of these artists.

In a short review of 'MacPherson, Shepherdson, Staunton', Dr Gertrude Langer got to the heart of the matter in a few lines: 'Collage, the technique more than any other that has stimulated creative twentieth-century ideas in art, can be used in *various* ways for *various* reasons.'[15] Staunton has always found her *own* reasons: meaningful resemblances to other artists' work are, in reality, reasonably few. What should be said about her practice and the way it was interpreted at the time, however, is well expressed in the text that accompanied the same exhibition.

> Madonna Staunton does not consciously strive to represent any particular themes or ideas in her work. She builds up each work relying on her feel for colour and design. Ideas on meaning evolve on reflection. As with poetry, the ideas expressed are open to interpretation . . . Staunton tries to avoid preconceived ideas, about what a collage should be and more specifically about what particular objects mean or used to mean. By so doing, she has managed to create a personal vision of great beauty and quiet charm.[16]

Painting without painting

Though this exhibition focuses on Staunton's painting practice, it is not intended to underplay the significance of her collage and assemblage works — the intent is to read those works as, or at least in close relation to, painting. This relationship is most easily recognised in her assemblages, for example *Assemblage with plank* 1988, acquired for the Queensland Art Gallery Collection in 1992. Iterating the 'painting without painting' theme, Staunton took a sizable and denuded canvas stretcher and created a composition by fixing to it a pair of folding chairs and a reclaimed house painter's scaffold board, complete with a cosmos of starlike splatters and cloudlike streaks of paint. The chance patterns evoke a sense of the timelessness of the cosmos, and similarly the chairs speak of time spent contemplating, as a painter might in front of their work. The presence of two chairs is an ambiguous invitation: it could imply an exchange, perhaps at remove, with an audience or another artist. Tucked behind one chair is a record cover for the album *Still Crazy After All These Years* (1976) by Paul Simon — and so it may be that the two chairs are to accommodate multiple aspects of the one: the artist. This dry, yet playful coda is lighter than Staunton's other artworks of the time that, paradoxically, reeked of emptiness.

In *Chair with packing case* 1993, now in the University of Queensland's collection, a single well-worn wooden chair has been camouflaged by the addition of recycled painted timber. Among the aged, flaked paint, the chair is at once hidden by, and also appears to be hiding in, the gesture. The work — alongside other key works also in this exhibition, *Hide 1* and *Hide 2* 2002, and *Romantic doubt* 2004 — featured in the important survey of established

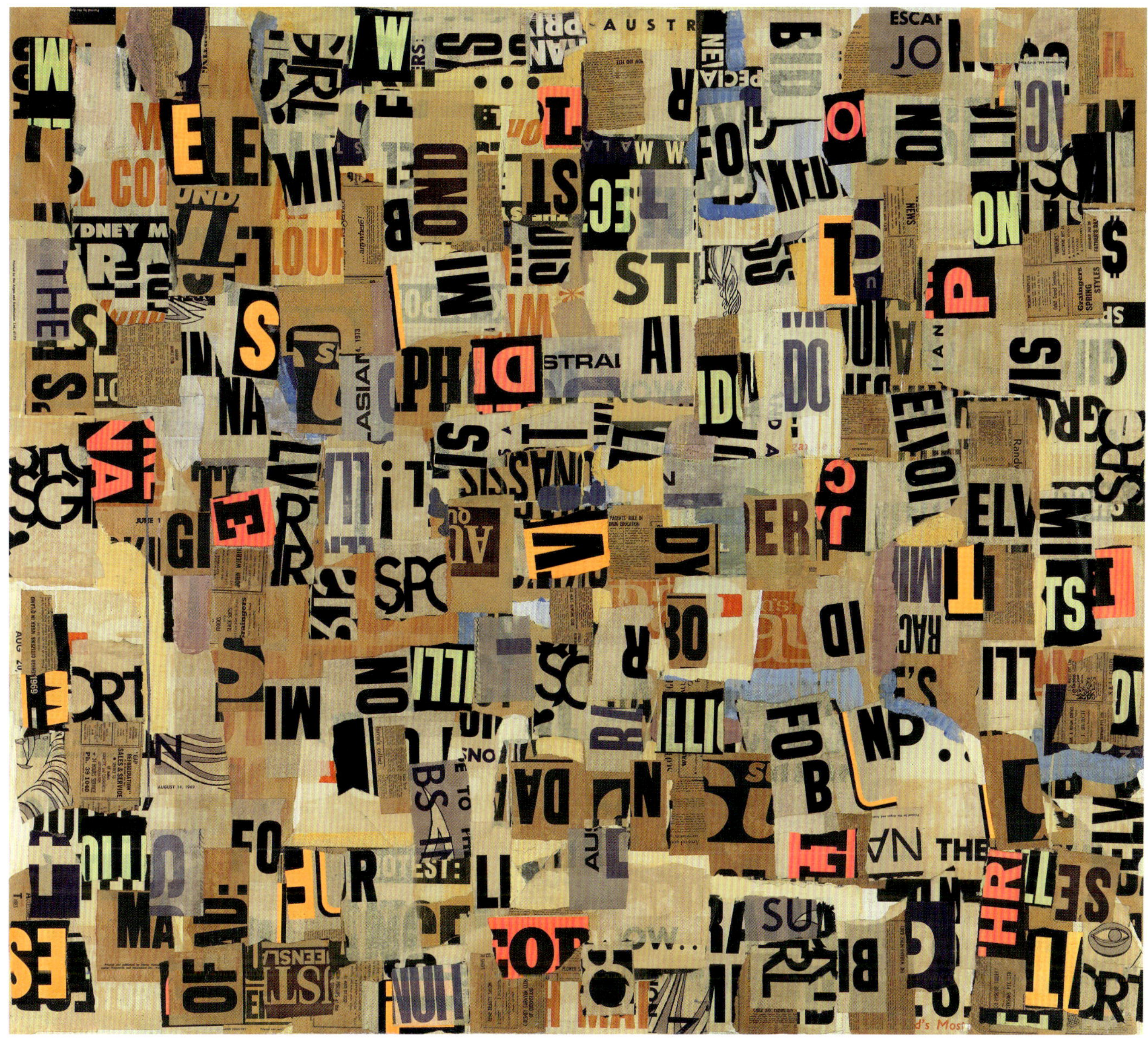

contemporary artists, 'Interesting Times' 2005, curated by Russell Storer for the Museum of Contemporary Art, Sydney. In the catalogue, Brisbane poet Nathan Shepherdson wrote about the artist's talent for engaging life, death and the echoes of presence in a single sign:

> Madonna Staunton has found a method of injecting philosophy into chairs. She hangs the coat of her thinking over the backs of them. The chairs she uses in her works are the timber ones. While timber is an inanimate substance, it should be remembered that we are sitting — or not sitting — on the flesh of trees. In profile a human being on a chair leaning over a table resembles a question mark. Perhaps the most pressing question Madonna asks of her chairs is if they can withstand the weight of absence.[17]

Untitled 1973
Paper collage on canvas
151 x 173cm
Purchased 1995. Queensland Art Gallery Foundation
Collection: Queensland Art Gallery

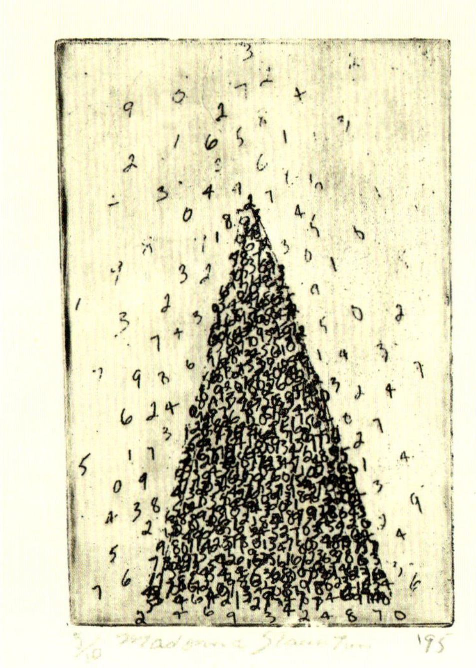

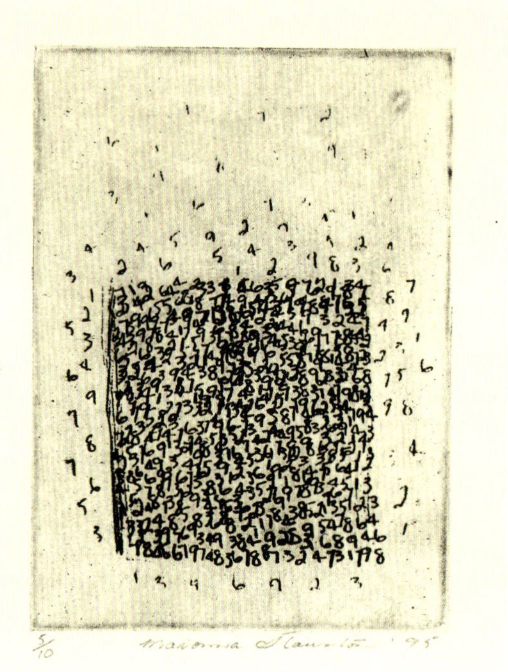

While Shepherdson's idea of wood being the flesh of trees may seem fanciful, it articulates both the depth of imagination and empathetic projection of the artist. Staunton's short story *The Small Garden* (1982) — republished in this volume — takes this fancy one step further to identify the fears of a shrub under the eye of a gardener. Shepherdson also implicates the balance between preservation, states of decay and regeneration, as well as different states of presence, both physical and remembered into the reading. *Hide 1* and *Hide 2* recall the tipi structure used by nomadic First Nations peoples of the United States, though Staunton's are somewhat more defence-armoured. Here, two ladders (perhaps once joined by the plank from *Assemblage with plank*) are covered with painted timber lengths to create a physical protection for the psyche.

Similarly, *Romantic doubt*, another painted timber assemblage, presents other ideas about escape through literature. Select timbers have been arranged rather like the artist's own overflowing bookshelves, along which Staunton has sporadically scribed the nouns 'UTOPIA' and 'EREHWON' — references to Sir Thomas More's *Utopia* (1516) and Samuel Butler's *Erewhon: or, Over the Range* (1872). In More's text, Utopia (derived from the Greek for 'no place') was a fictional, idyllic community created for the purpose of indicating and imagining a different existence apart from the status quo. Inspired by the author's time in New Zealand, Butler's *Erewhon*, an anagram of nowhere, satirises the scattering British Empire and is a kind of early treatise on the potential for 'machine consciousness', otherwise known as artificial intelligence. Perhaps in this work, we can see the artist doubting her 'romantic' belief in positive evolution and the direction of her society in general. Ideas become cluttered and counterproductive — invoked, though shuttered out.

Untitled (triangle) 1995
Etching, ed. 5/10
14 x 10.5cm

Untiled (square) 1995
Etching, ed. 5/10
14 x 10.5cm

Collection: The artist

Numbers game 2002 speaks of a different kind of alienation: that of being misunderstood and typecast. Comprised of redundant railway markers, complete with coding and small ink bottles, *Numbers game* resembles a Rosalie Gascoigne gridded reflective road-sign work, jumbled, or even exploded. Tired of being discussed in reference to Gascoigne, Staunton composed an

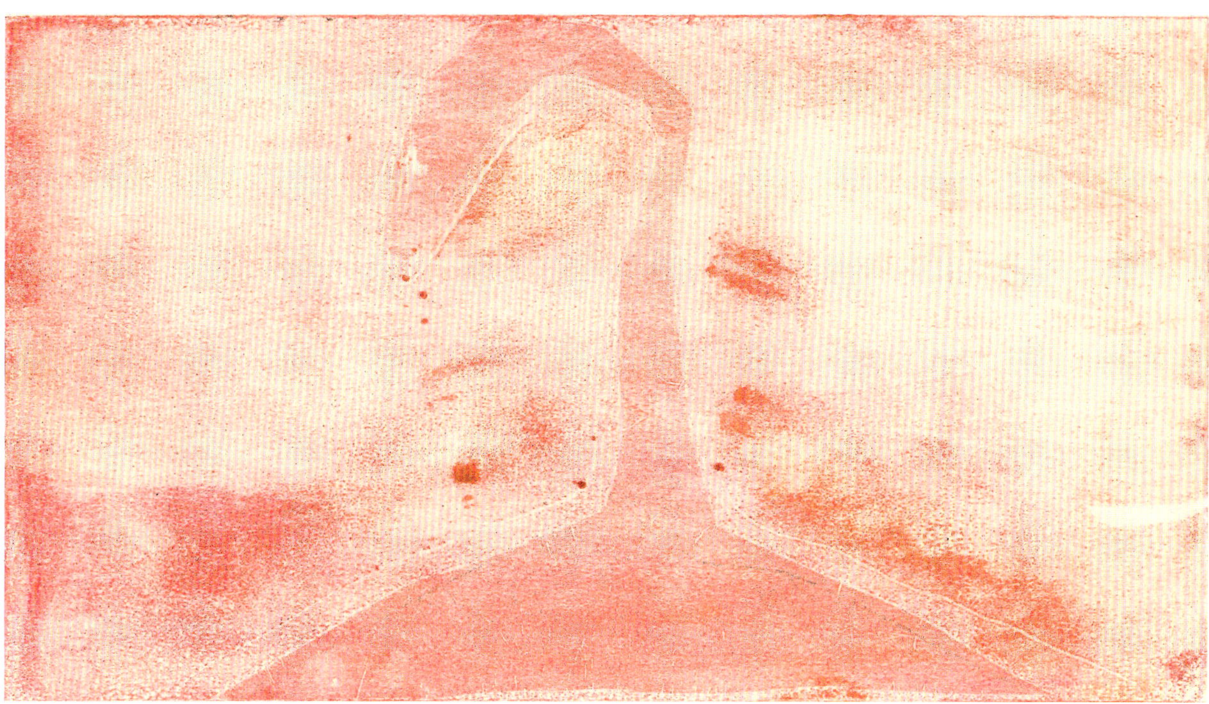

arrangement as if it had been shook in frustration. For her, numbers and letters are important symbols associated with the systematic denial of rights among certain citizens by authoritarian regimes. Even as a benign administrative process, the impersonal experience of being reduced to a number can sit at odds with a strong sense of self and self-worth. This process of divorcing or stripping identity is a practice that art critic Ihor Holubisky noted 'has the effect of desensitising and dehumanising' those citizens who are already the most disenfranchised. The Nazis were known for tattooing concentration camp detainees so that bodies of prisoners could be accounted for, either dead or alive.[18] Similar practices were inflicted on Indigenous Australians with King plates, used by colonists to identify leaders while also establishing a hierarchy and bureaucracy amid colonised populations. Later, *Immigrant* 2008, a tender graphic portrayal of Staunton's Irish forebears, would mark her concern for those who travel from a desperate situation (to another). The numbers in *Key*, also from 2002, would seem to reference the domestic and a longing for safety in the empty space behind a table leg. *Key* also references Staunton's interest in music and the qualities that are shared across visual and musical composition including tone, sequence and pace.

Painting with paint

Concurrently, Staunton had begun working with wire coathangers. Though coathangers seemed to represent a peculiar interest in the incidental to many of her admirers at the time, their significance becomes clear when tracing back through her later works. In her 'Armatures' series of 1999, she attached wire coathangers to pre-painted boards in an even dispersion, and then painted around them with a gestural action. In one respect they were a kind of painting system with set parameters, offering a safe process by which to return to painting *with* paint — but they also coded a personal insight. Rex Butler wrote an observant review of the work when it first showed at Bellas Gallery, contextualising the strategy with the shaped canvases of Frank Stella and Minimalism generally, but the real insight lay in his title, 'Ghosts in the closet'.[19]

Nodding bird c.1999
Relief print
14 x 25.5cm
Collection: The artist

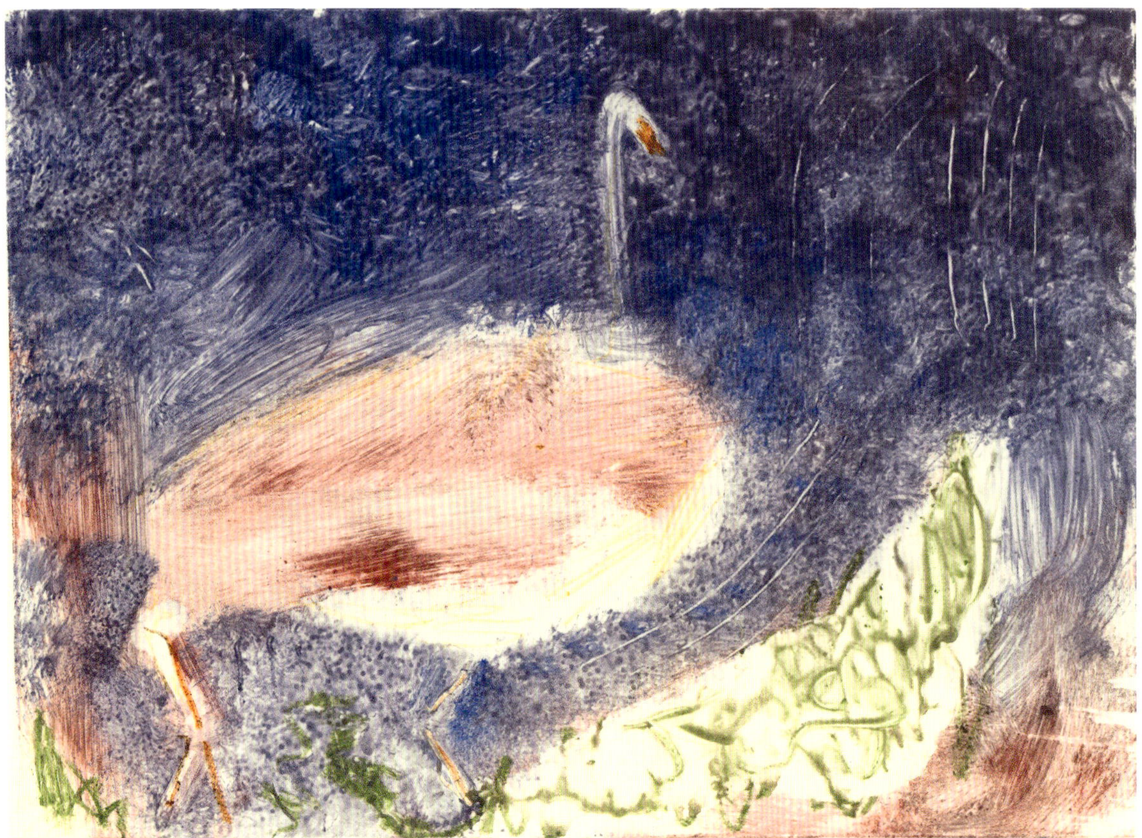

Staunton was thinking about the armour that we cloak ourselves in before we leave the home each day to face the world. Equally, she was also considering the restless aspects of ourselves — our sensitivities, vulnerabilities, secrets and compassion — that we might leave behind in the closet like coathangers, or skeletons, left to rattle. Perhaps we take the coat in order to leave the warmth of our souls behind.

Around this time, Staunton began making monotypes with the printing assistance of Wim de Vos. As stated earlier, the fast-paced process with its potential for delicate tonalities suited Staunton perfectly. Her first subjects were simple line drawings, again of coathangers, and then of safety pins. Safety pins are useful devices — though with a tendency to prick when least expected — and exert a kind of karmic justice that balances their brilliant utility. Soon, these simple illustrations began to morph into whimsical scenes. Coathangers became birds, and safety pins found themselves in idyllic garden settings: life was everywhere in everything. A parallel practice worth bearing in mind might be that of the American poet Gary Snyder, whom Staunton has met and admires. Snyder has a strong belief in the place of environmental and cultural ecology in the face of globalist expansion; he is known for his profound interest in the role and experience of community, and his respect for diverse cultures including Buddhism, the ancient Chinese poets, and First Nations across America. In his writing he often addresses interconnectedness, the life of things, and the careless pressures exerted on the world by the powerful or inattentive — in much the same way Staunton does.

Monotype (Mother bird) c.1999
Monotype
15.5 x 22cm
Collection: The artist

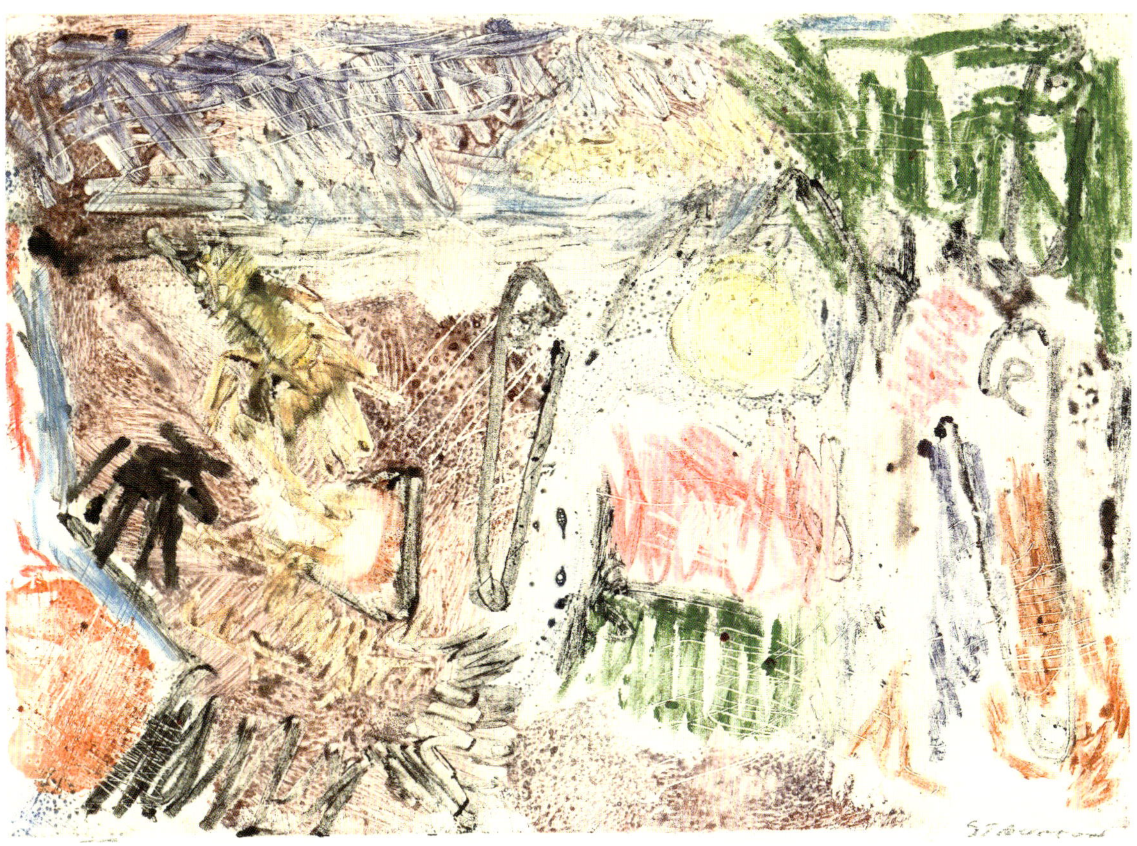

After the World Trade Center attack in New York on 11 September 2001, the artist's empathy for those involved drew her monotypes into yet darker territory. In the 'Sept. 11' series, two dark book-like blocks of ink appeared page after page, interrupted by the ghostly trails of her hand falling down the plate. These haunting gestures recall the victims who fell hundreds of metres in front of the dark plate glass, and in front of the rest of the world as it watched the shocking broadcast together at once.

It seems that faced with this terrible reminder of mortality, along with the more subtle variations in self that aging delivers, Staunton gained a new clarity, daring and vitality. Her work took on a narrative dimension of sorts, though she carefully strived to avoid being didactic. The artist continued making monotypes through c.2005, expanding her subjects, particularly still life, and experimenting with strategies of representation until she made a wholehearted return to figurative painting.

Among the most accomplished paintings of this new period is *Reprise* c.2007. Here, an elongated figure, painted in murky tones worthy of Walter Sickert, stares out at the viewer with a brittle and nervous exhaustion. The subject's face seems to hover in front of her head, detached as it rests in her hand in a way that suggests they have been charting the formless, infinite void of depression. The eyes, marked with disbelief and acceptance, strike out. Later works *They say* 2010 and *No one said* 2010, while continuing the investigation into (self–)portraiture, refer clearly to brooding feelings surrounding family inheritance. *The reader* 2012, depicts a head in a book — the preferred means of escape — and the colour of the mood that is felt in this limbo of residing in the physical world but being present in another.

Monotype (Landscape with safety pin)
c.1999
Monotype
16 x 22cm
Collection: The artist

In *Anxiety* 2012 a sole figure is nearly ejected from the picture plane, tumbling out of this synthetic space, preoccupied and faltering. Many of Staunton's compositions are articulated in a condensed geometric arrangement — a post-cubist strategy linked to her tonal collage, but coded with emotional sensitivity provoked by the wrestling of humanist ideals and hostile circumstance. Brilliant, piercing blue eyes strike here too, out of an astonishingly sophisticated composition of layered complementary tones — pink, yellow, mauve and more blue — all worked over each other with a delicate brush action. The figure's hands seem to repel each other like magnets of matching polarity, signifying a body and mind in all-consuming turmoil.

In an effort to exert some order over chaos, Staunton attempted to frame her future after death as she optimistically aims to experience it. Her 'Postcard' series addresses authors and musicians already passed. In writing to Samuel Beckett, Emily Dickinson, Franz Kafka, Tiny Tim and English poet Stevie Smith,[20] she announces her resolve to locate them, finding consolation in a kind of transcendental goal setting. These novel projections are couched in a brutally honest personal reflection about the limits of life and the ideas that have made it worthwhile, charging the work with startling sensitivity and intelligence. Cats have steadily featured in other recent works, and Staunton's insight into and admiration for their fine-tuned engagement with their surrounds is clear. Their emotions are absolute and their habitats are lively. For them, time is measured differently, and each moment is valued and lived with equal verve, whether ranging or resting. Cats might make the finest Buddhists.

On first view, this heavy atmosphere seems to have lifted a little further in *Out of a clear blue sky* 2013. Its glorious sense of sunlight and blue sky could easily be mistaken for an optimistic statement. Of course, the idiom is not about the parting of the clouds to receive the gifts of chance — but instead describes an unexpected injury sustained somehow out of nowhere. Even in the finest moments lurks hazard. Similarly bittersweet, *Sunflowers* 2013 is remarkable for its economy of form. Again post-cubist, but with a nod to Vincent van Gogh, Staunton has constructed a deceptively simple composition full of the pulse of nature, tempered by a mindfulness of the inevitable decay of all life. While Staunton would declare a still life like this a mere 'busy work' while she waits for greater inspiration, its ambience reveals her immense capacity for colour and form in painting, and indicates an abundance of melancholy insights present in its making and in the artist.

Madonna Staunton's story is a lesson in an individual's capacity to change and adapt, to reintroduce and renew, and to persevere in the shadows when necessary. It might be that a small revolution in the artist's thinking took place at some stage along the way, yet on careful viewing it seems that her path has remained relatively true. Needless to say, travel far enough in any one direction and there is bound to be a change in aspect. Together, this group of works represents many of Madonna Staunton's key achievements in an eventful lifetime — with still more to come. They demonstrate the importance of investing, for the longest term, in ideas and ideals, feelings and thoughts. Expressed with talents amassed over a career spanning nearly 50 years, each work, however humble, attests to the insight that can come with age and profound reflection. Having mastered the ability to create compositions analogous to states of meditation or inner harmony by a pattern of particularly sympathetic aesthetic ordering, Staunton then had the wit and wherewithal to reveal more and more of her personal experiences than would have previously been concealed. Her deep expressive content and thoroughgoing philosophical understanding of human existence is now exposed, unprotected. Attracted to this wisdom, it appears that what Staunton had been looking for from the start, found her in the end.

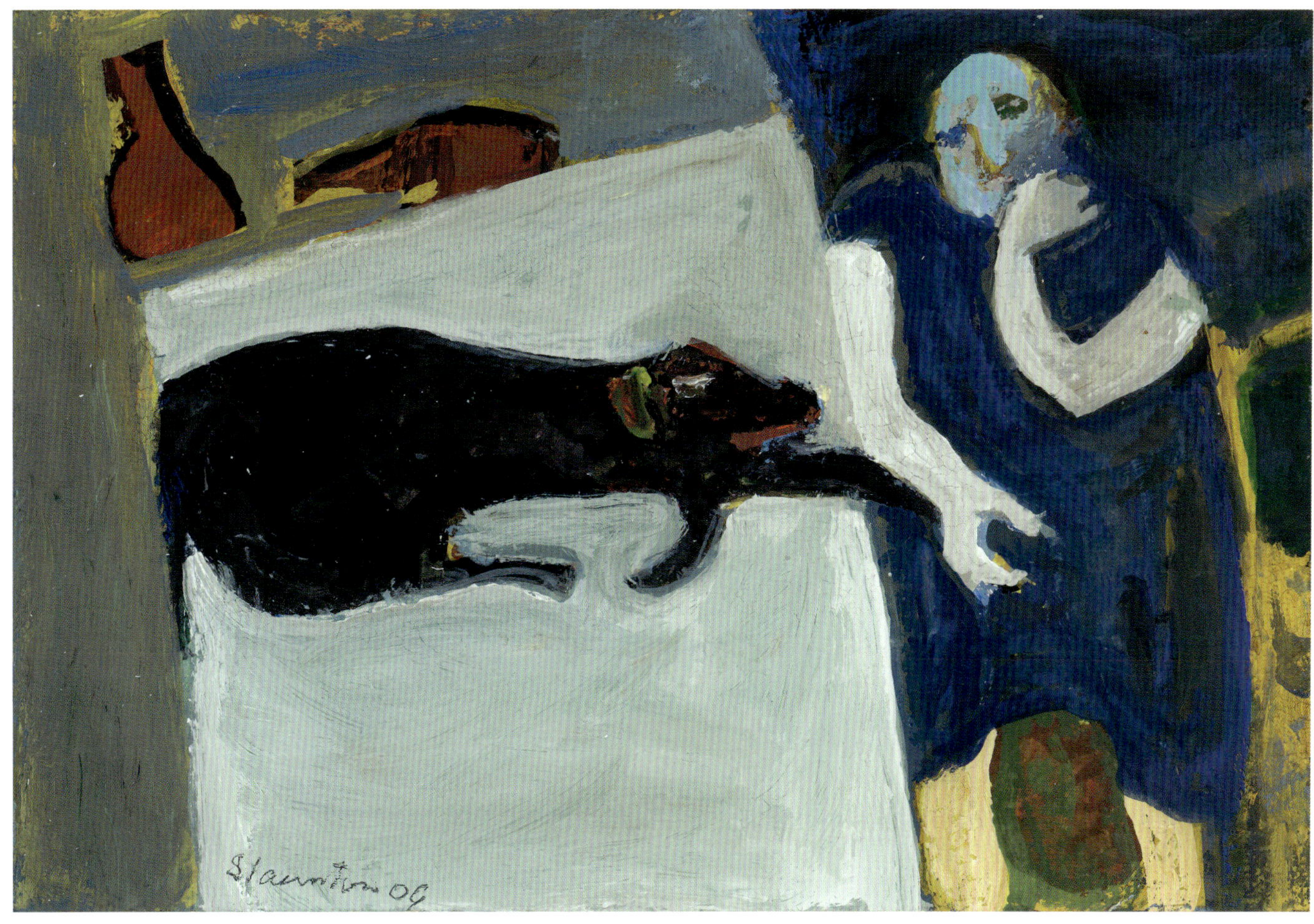

1 Madonna Staunton suggested in a discussion with Josh Milani that until her reengagement with representational painting she had been 'hiding in formalism'. This can be taken to mean that the artist was concealing certain observations into works that might have appeared exclusively occupied with aesthetic concerns, and also that she herself had been hiding behind the idea that she was a 'formalist' artist who dealt in the relationship between colour, tone, shape, scale, texture. 18 June 2013.

2 Stephen Rainbird, in *Madonna Staunton: A Survey 1966–1993*, Queensland University of Technology, Brisbane, 1994, p.21.

3 Discussion with the artist 8 March 2014.

4 Helen Fridemanis in *Artists and Aspects of the Contemporary Art Society, Queensland Branch*, Boolarong Publications, Bowen Hills, Brisbane, 1991, p.118.

5 Michele Helmrich, 'A Poetics of Discipline: Madonna Staunton' in *Madonna Staunton: A Survey 1966–1993*, p.7.

6 Frank J MacHovec (trans.), *The Book of Tao*, The Peter Pauper Press, New York, 1962, pp.39–40.

7 Rainbird, p.21.

8 Fridemanis, p.145.

9 Roy Churcher, artist and teacher, briefly instructed Staunton during her time at Central Technical College in 1964. Fridemanis, p.23.

10 Fridemanis, p.121.

11 Urszula Szulakowska, *Experimental Art in Queensland, 1975–1995: An Introductory Study*, Griffith Uni Print, Griffith University, Brisbane, 1998, p.VI.

12 Fridemanis, p121.

13 David Andre, *MacPherson, Shepherdson, Staunton*, University Art Museum, University of Queensland, Brisbane, 1979, unpaginated.

14 Szulakowska, p.16.

15 Dr Gertrude Langer, 'Making their mark', *Courier-Mail*, Brisbane, 28 July 1979.

16 Andre, unpaginated.

17 Nathan Shepherdson in *Interesting Times: Focus on Contemporary Australian Art*, Russell Storer, Museum of Contemporary Australian Art, Sydney, 2005, p.125.

18 Ihor Holubizky, 'Madonna Staunton: sorting through ... organising things, in time ... through time' in Michael Snelling (ed.), *Madonna Staunton*, IMA Publishing, Brisbane, 2003, p.22.

19 Rex Butler, 'Ghosts in the closet', *Courier-Mail*, 15 August 1998.

20 A great coincidence, Smith was raised by an aunt named Madge, and resented her absent father though this atypical family space offered her an independence that would be the foundation of her attitude and work. Her most famous poem is 'Not waving but drowning', and much of her work dealt with death and depression.

Kitchen blues 2009
Gouache
9.8 x 14.8cm
Collection: Michael and Kylie Rayner, Brisbane

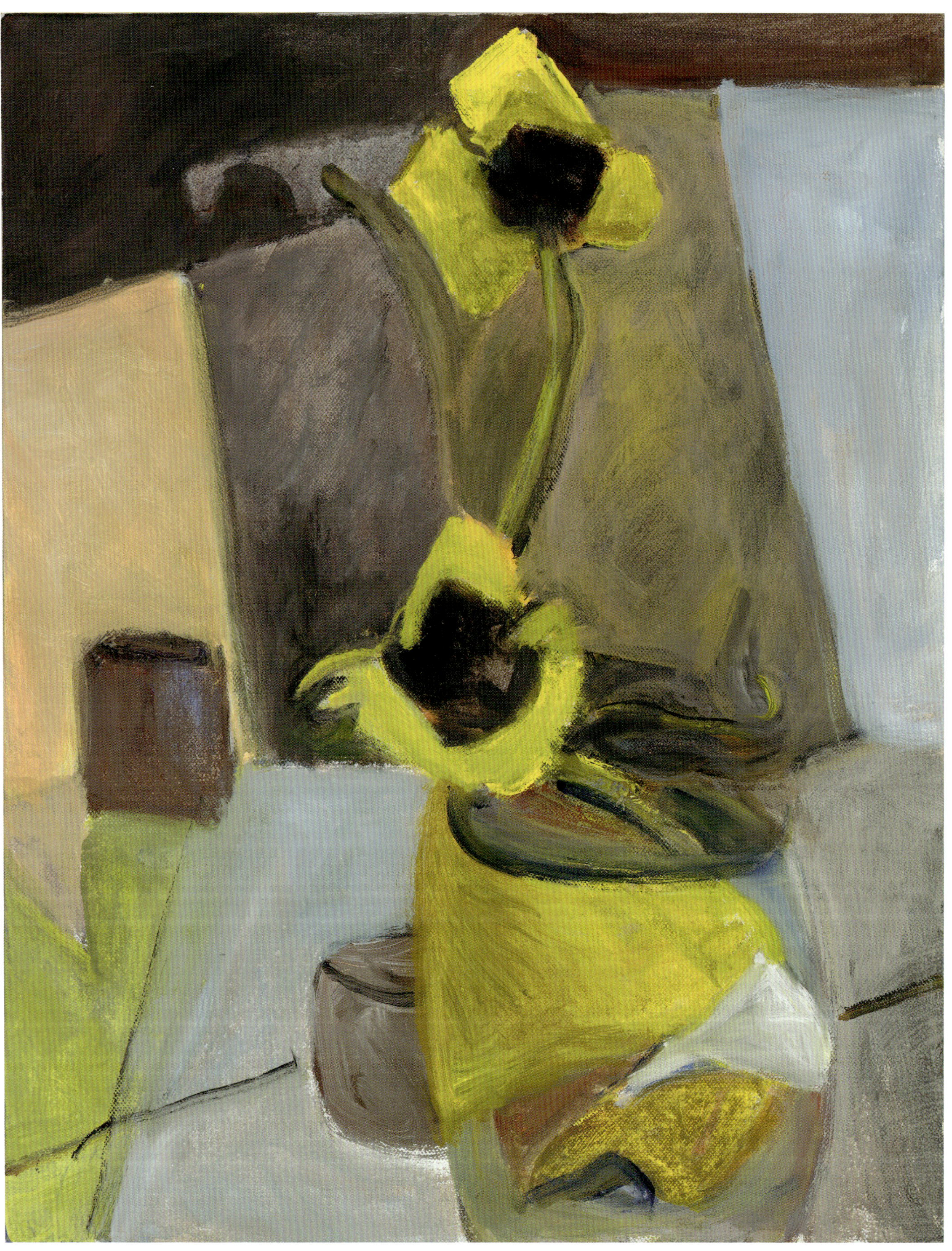

THE SMALL GARDEN

Madonna Staunton

I introduce myself at one as a garden edging, not more than sixteen centimetres in height, a small evergreen shrub. I form an enclosure, but don't feel the presence of a house, people rarely move around the area which I cover. Perhaps, I am flanked by a cemetery, one of those new lawn cemeteries where the gravestones are laid out like so many door mats. Some, I hear, are supplied with fresh flowers but I suspect my plots are mainly the repository for the leavings of cats and dogs or occasionally an uncomfortable chaise-longue for lovers. Not that I am aware of much in the way of such happenings as I have limited appraisal from my small vantage point.

I sometimes wonder how a small herbaceous growth like myself developed the faculty of reflection. In the gospels of Jesus Christ lilies and small birds are chosen to illustrate stories in parables but were unaware of their selfhood and merely acted as symbols to point up a truth. But for myself, it is different, I know my height to be so much and my appearance to be green and bushy. Like any conscious being I know where I begin and where I leave off.

One day a gardener came and stood looking down at me. I knew him to be a gardener because he carried a pair of shears and wiped his forehead often as though he had spent some time at a physical task. I felt afraid and drew in my stems and leaves in case he began to trim and alter my appearance. I knew pain as well as my ability to reflect, and even vanity entered into the fear of those shears, pointed and sharp like the bill of a large bird. After standing a while gazing around he moved away and I gave a sigh which rippled along the whole length of me, for I had no ambition to enclose a rose garden or some gothic folly, or even a piece of sculpture fashioned by man's anxiety. I was free of all 'noblesse oblige', and whole in myself. My corners might have been calculated by a scientist, my geometry was exact and beautiful. I wanted above all to be left in peace, alone with my wonderings and speculations, contented as a child folding a square of paper to make a paper plane.

Originally published in *Colours of Camouflage*, SweetWater Poets, Wavell Heights, 1982, p.17.

Sunflowers 2013
Synthetic polymer paint on canvas
51 x 40.5cm; 56 x 45.5 x 5cm (framed)
Purchased 2014 with funds from the Estate of the late Kathleen Elizabeth Mowle through the Queensland Art Gallery | Gallery of Modern Art Foundation
Collection: Queensland Art Gallery

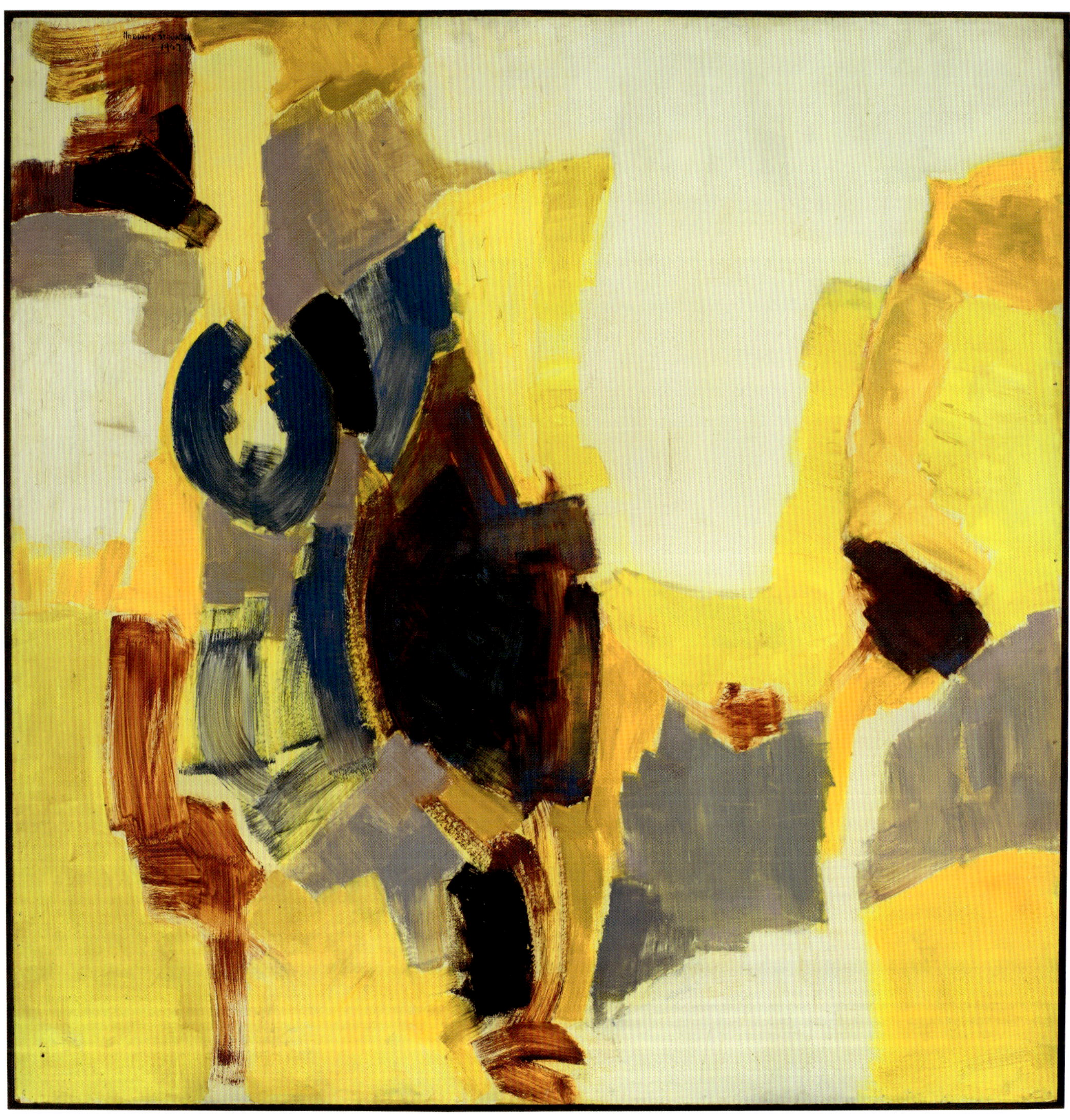

Easter 1967
Oil on composition board
122 x 122cm; 123.4 x 123.6 x 3.5cm (framed)
Gift of the artist, 1992
Queensland University of Technology Art Collection, Brisbane
Photograph: Carl Warner

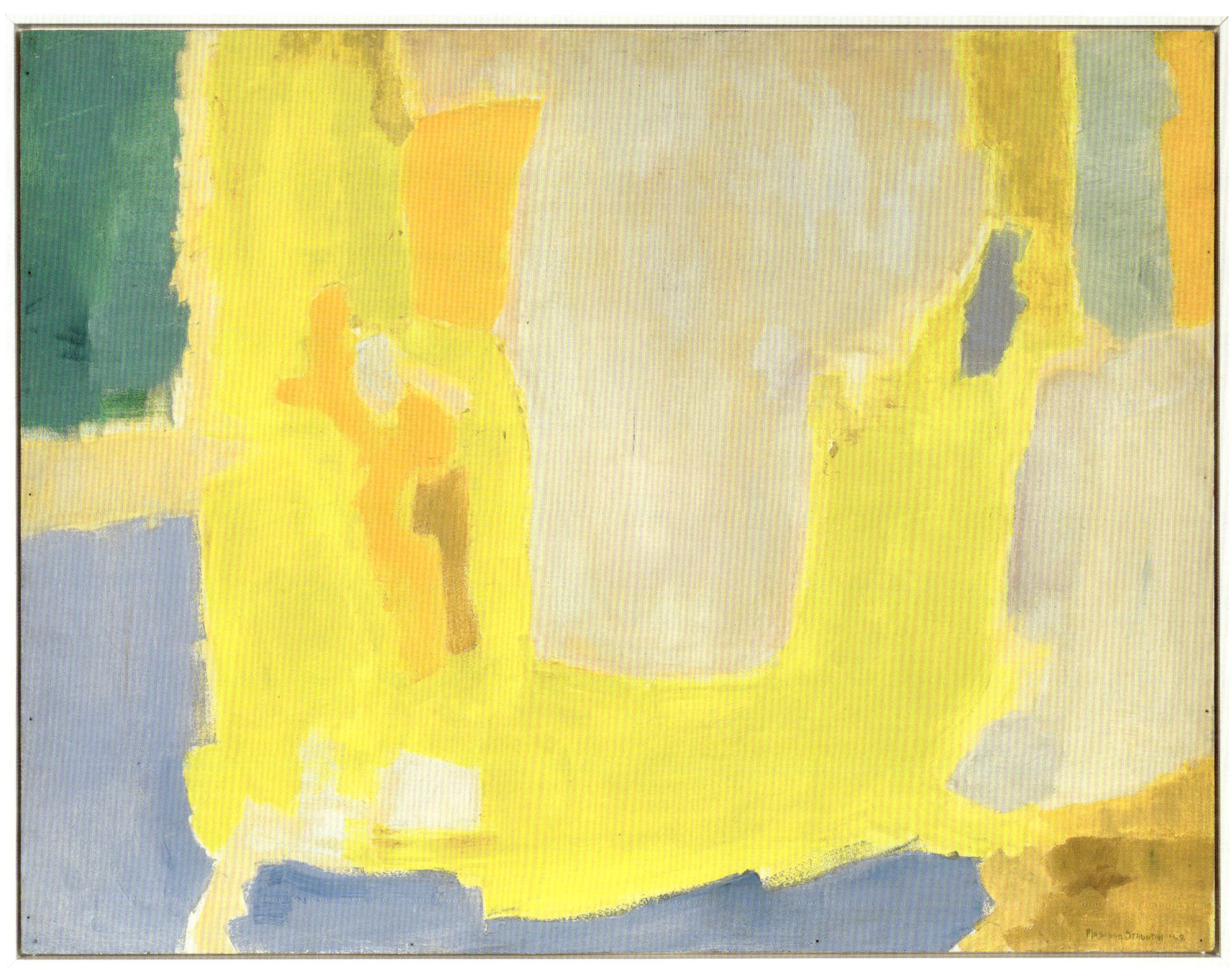

Peripheral green, blue 1968
Oil and synthetic polymer paint on composition board
91.5 x 122cm; 94.8 x 125 x 3.5cm (framed)
Private collection, Brisbane

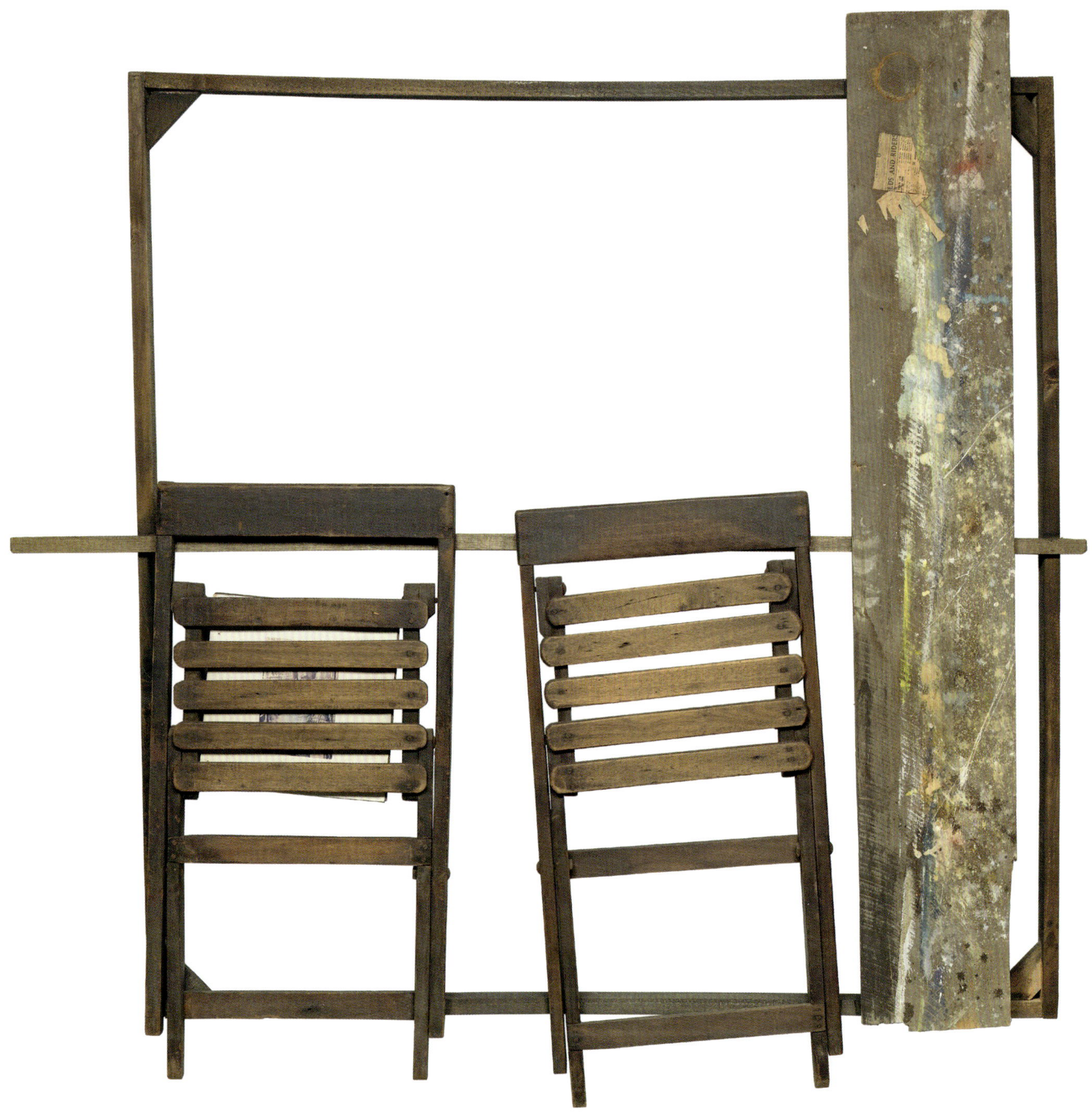

Assemblage with plank 1988
Wood, card, paint and paper
152 x 179 x 13.5cm (irreg.)
Purchased 1992
Collection: Queensland Art Gallery

Chair with packing case 1993
Painted wood and metal
110 x 74 x 45.5 cm (irreg.)
Purchased 2000.
Collection: University of Queensland, Brisbane
Photograph: Carl Warner

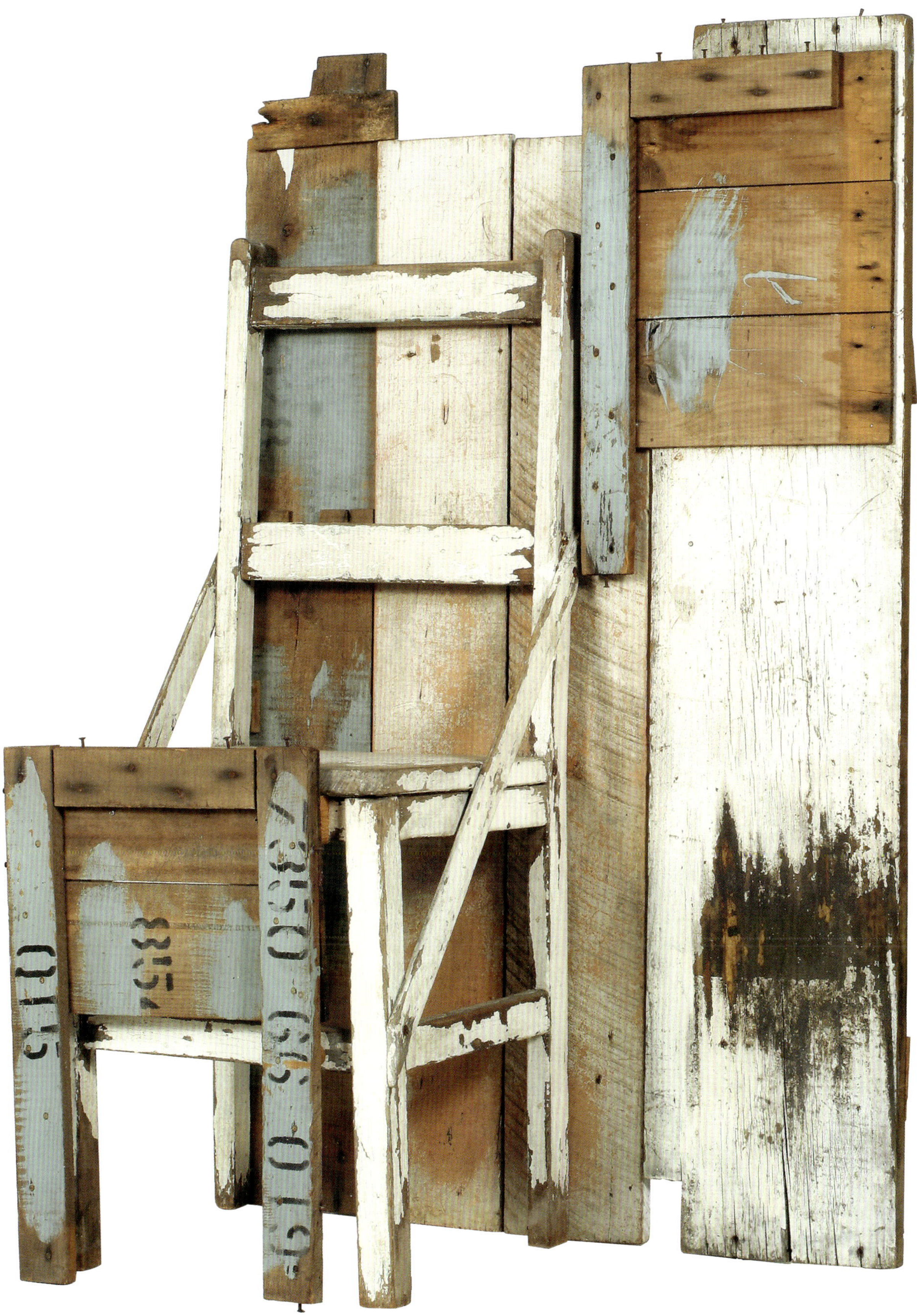

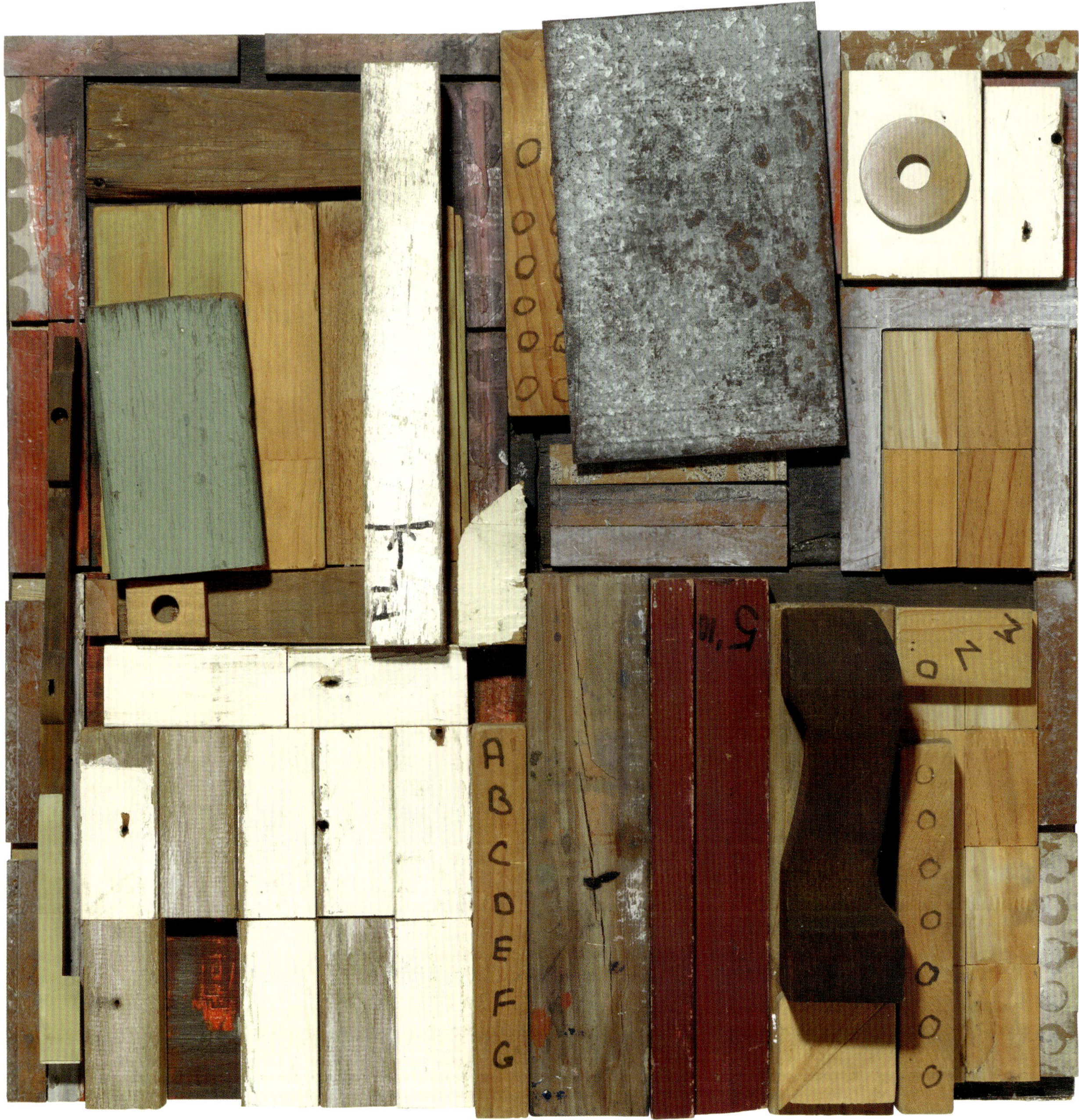

Romantic doubt 2004
Painted wood, wood, metal, synthetic polymer paint, ink and glue on composition board
3 units: 61 x 61 16.5cm; 61.5 x 61.4 x 11cm; 62 x 66 x 11cm (irreg.)
Private collection

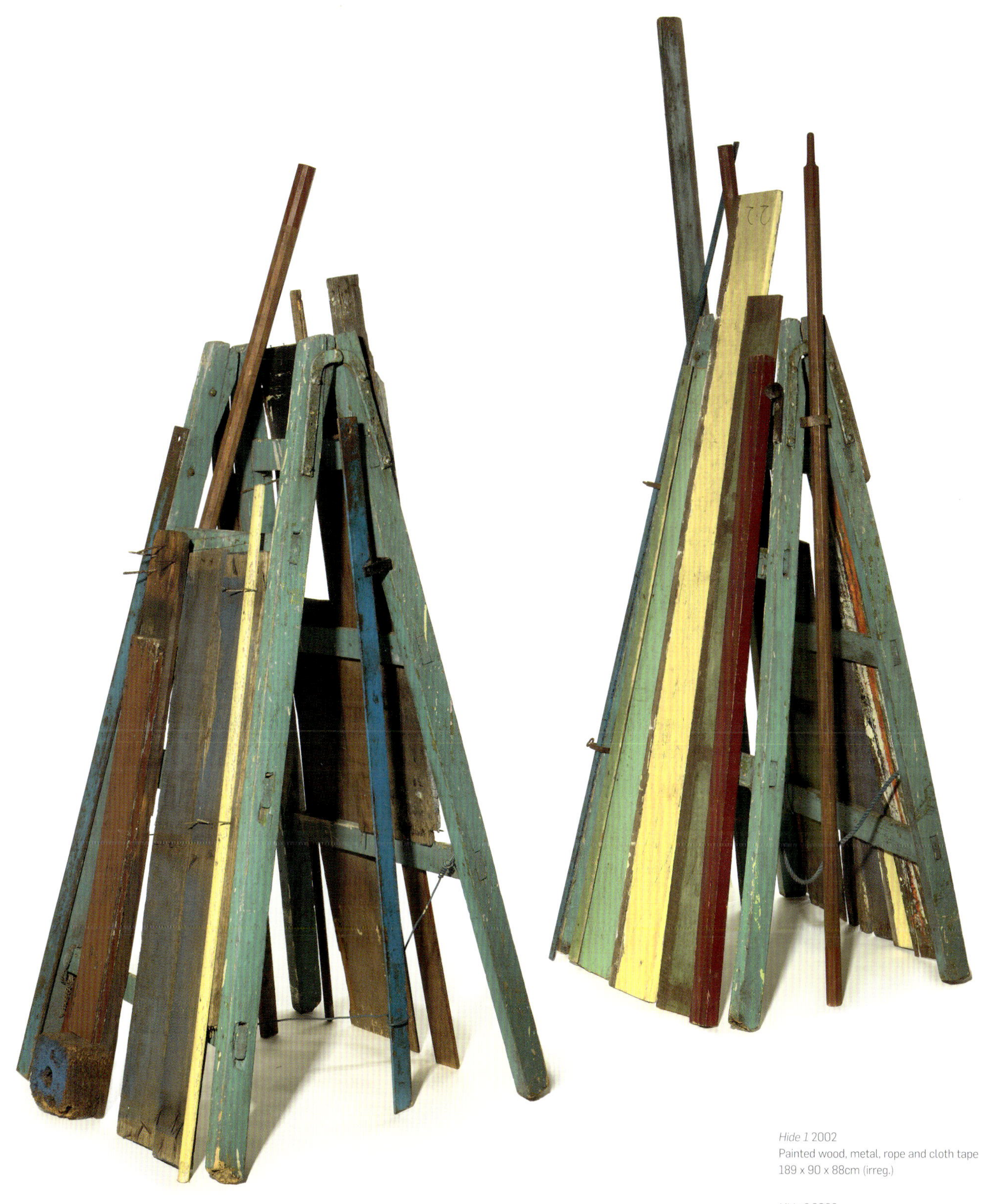

Hide 1 2002
Painted wood, metal, rope and cloth tape
189 x 90 x 88cm (irreg.)

Hide 2 2002
Painted wood, metal, rope and cloth tape
227 x 82 x 78cm (irreg.)

Collection: The artist

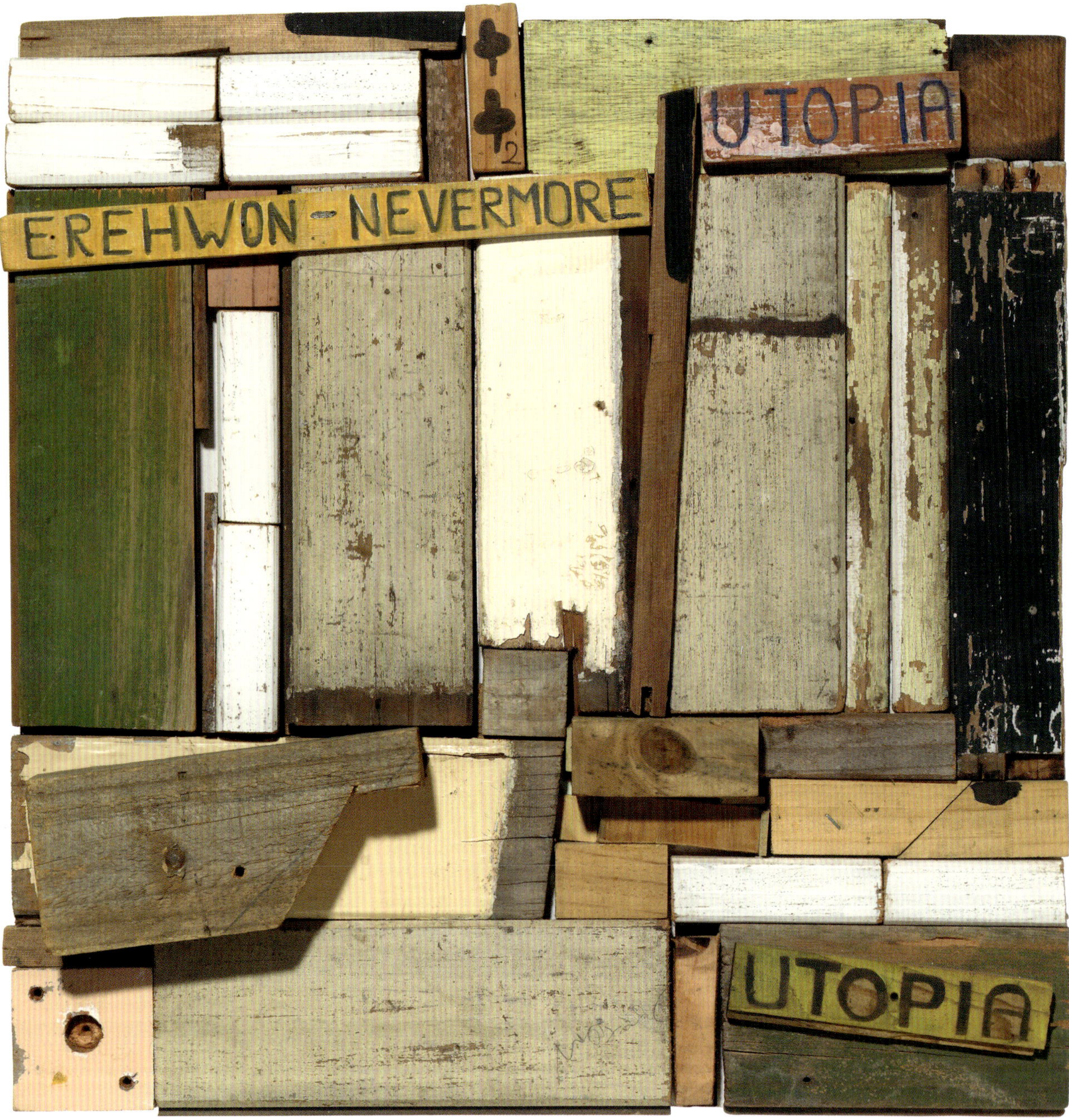
UTOPIA
ERЕHWON - NEVERMORE
UTOPIA

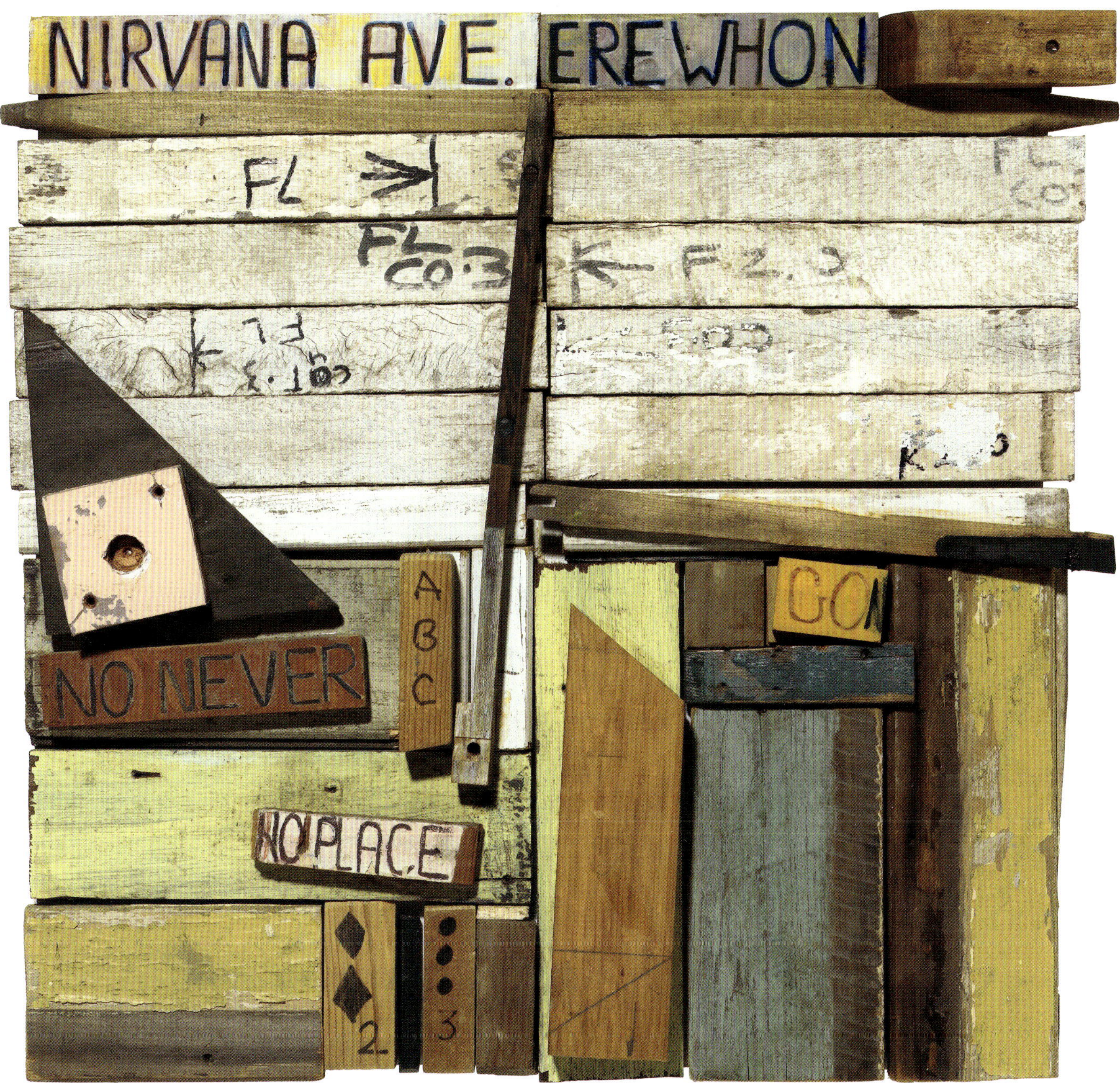
NIRVANA AVE.
EREWHON
NO NEVER
ABC
GO
NO PLACE
2
3

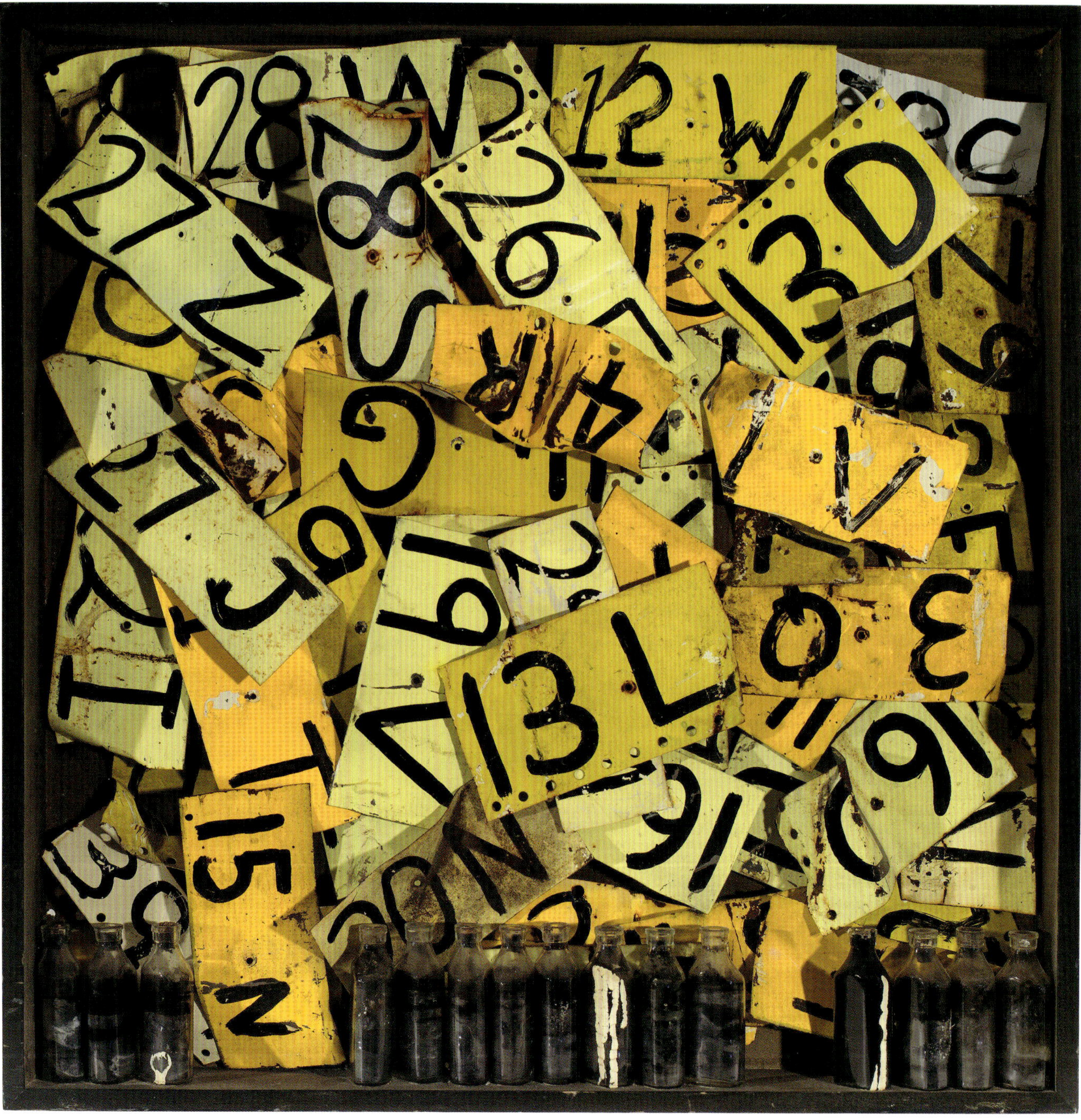

Numbers game 2002
Painted metal, ink bottles
and timber box
90 x 90 x 10cm
Purchased 2006 through the
Betty Quelhurst Fund
Queensland University of Technology Art
Collection, Brisbane
Photograph: Carl Warner

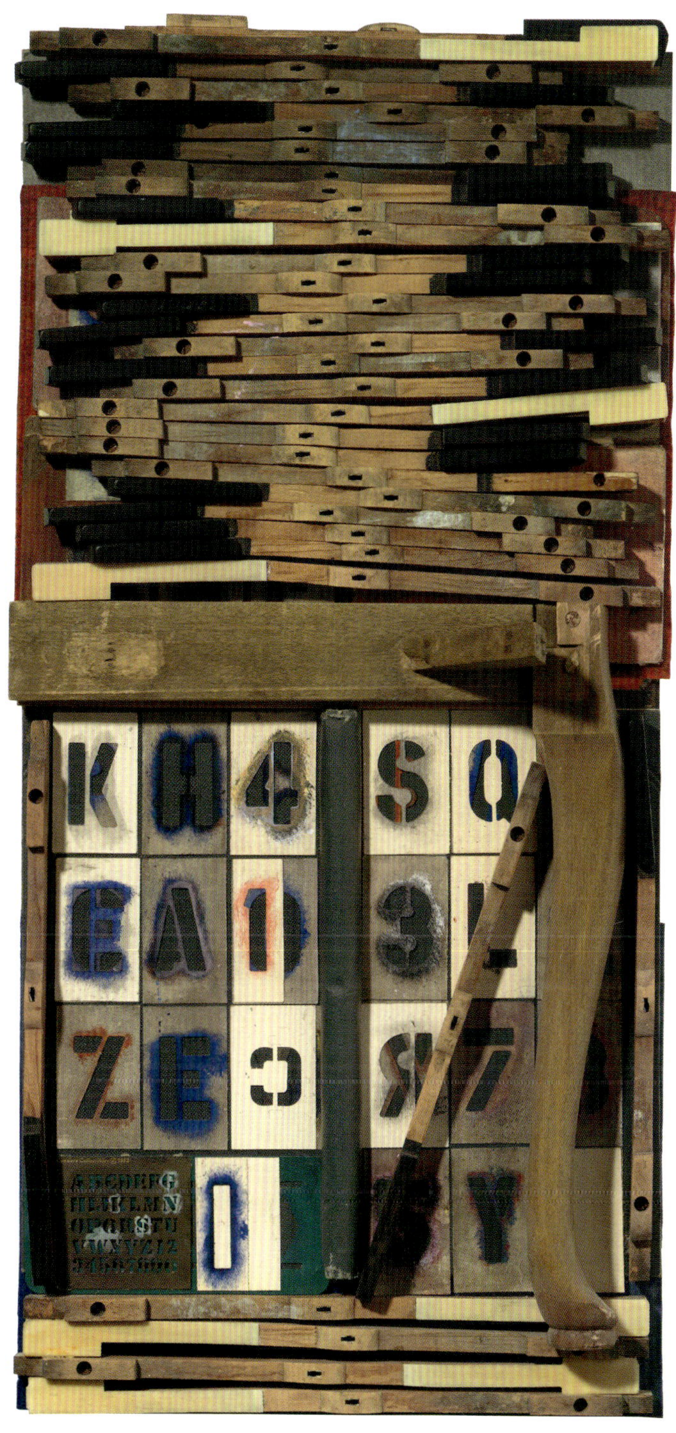

Key 2002
Wood, card, felt, metal, plastic, cloth-bound card and synthetic polymer paint on composition board
84 x 40.8 x 9.2cm (irreg.)
Collection: Michael and Kylie Rayner, Brisbane

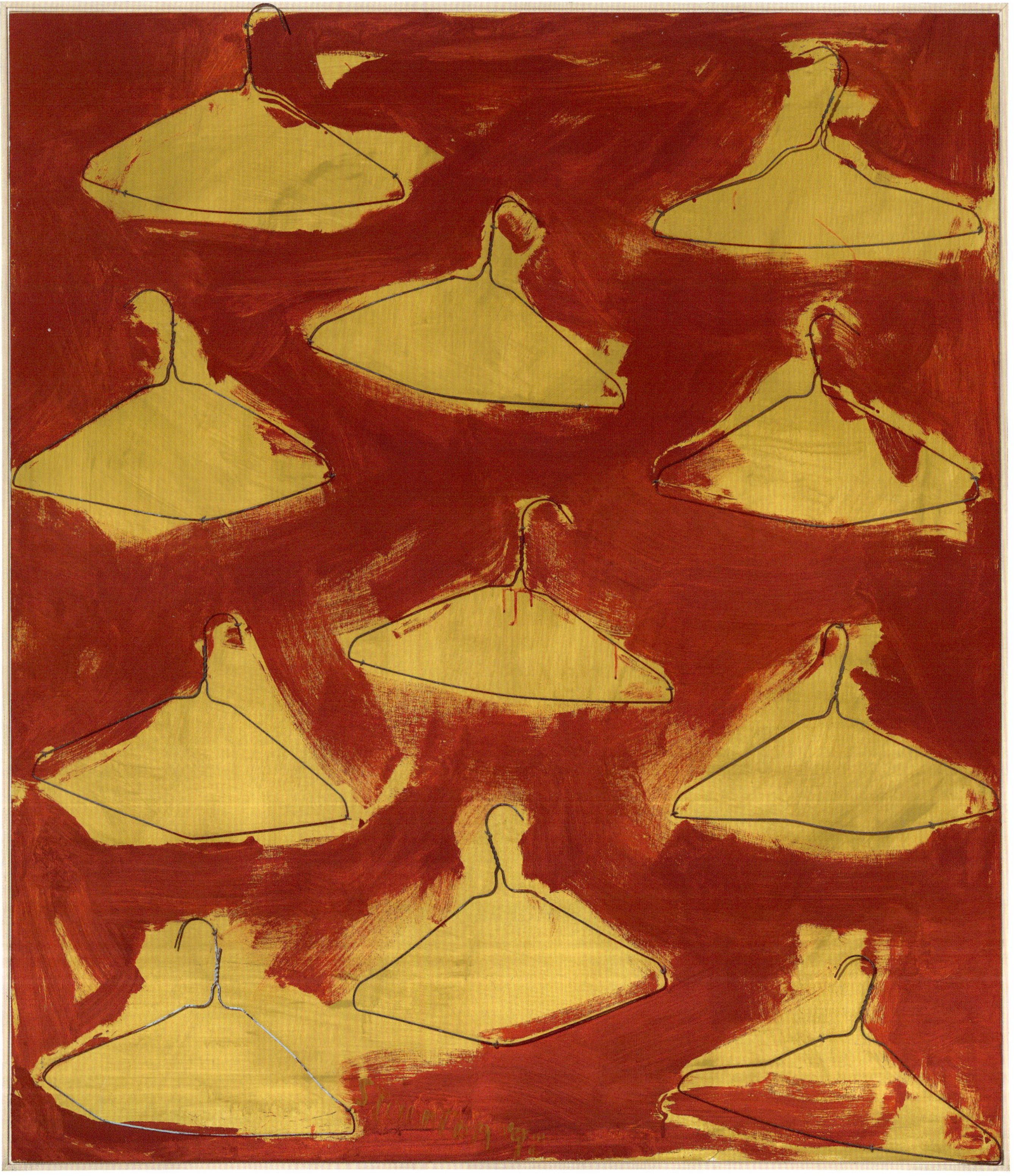

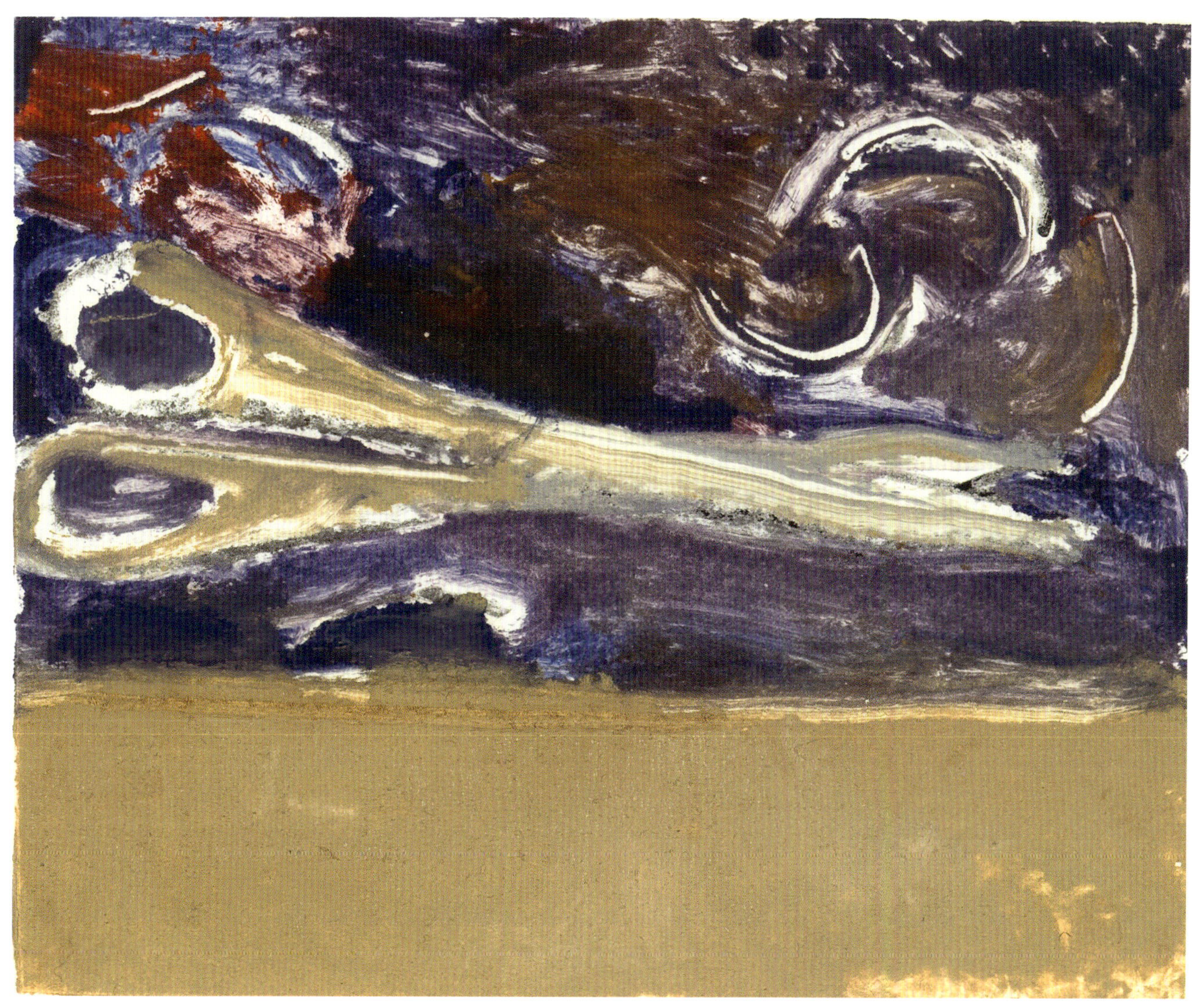

Armature 2 1999
Synthetic polymer paint
and wire on plywood
138.3 x 122.4cm (irreg.): 140 x 124.5cm x
5.5cm (framed)

Floating lovers no.2 c.2005
Monotype
10 x 13cm

Collection: The artist

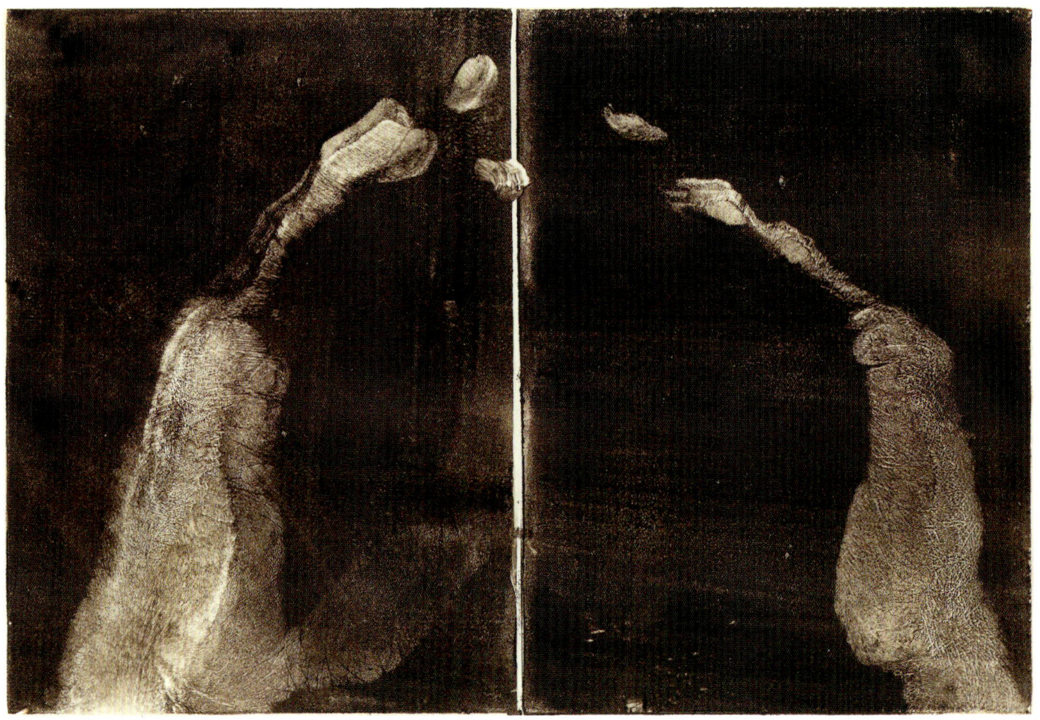

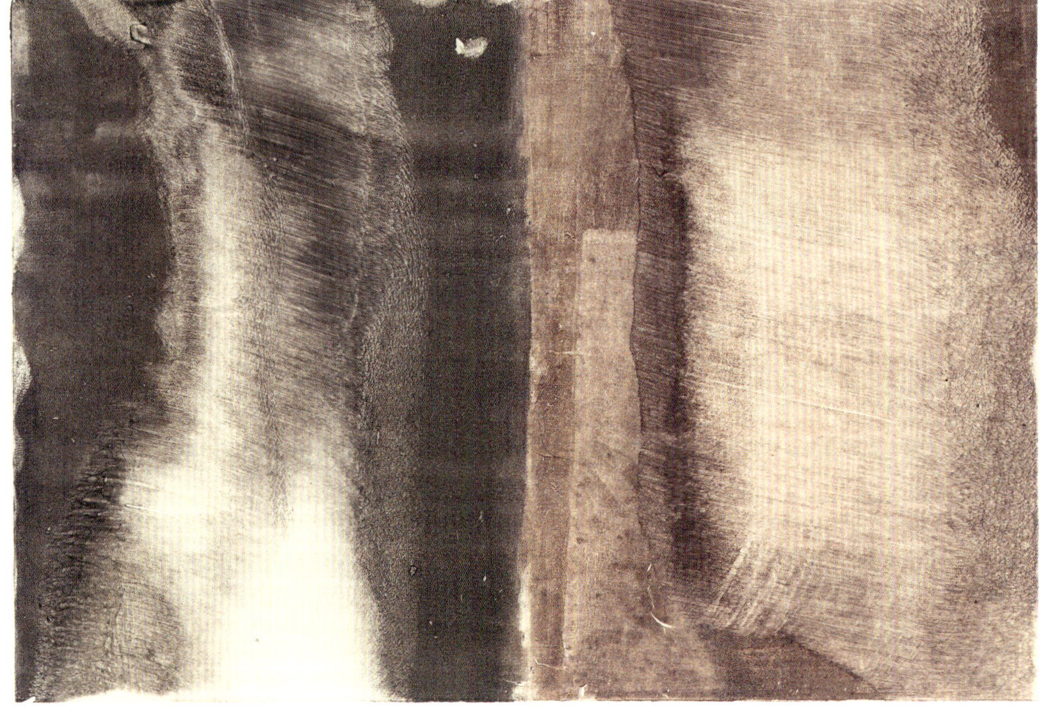

N.Y. 11 Sept 01 2001
Monotype
16 x 24.5cm

N.Y. 11 Sept 01 2001
Monotype
16 x 24.5cm

Collection: The artist

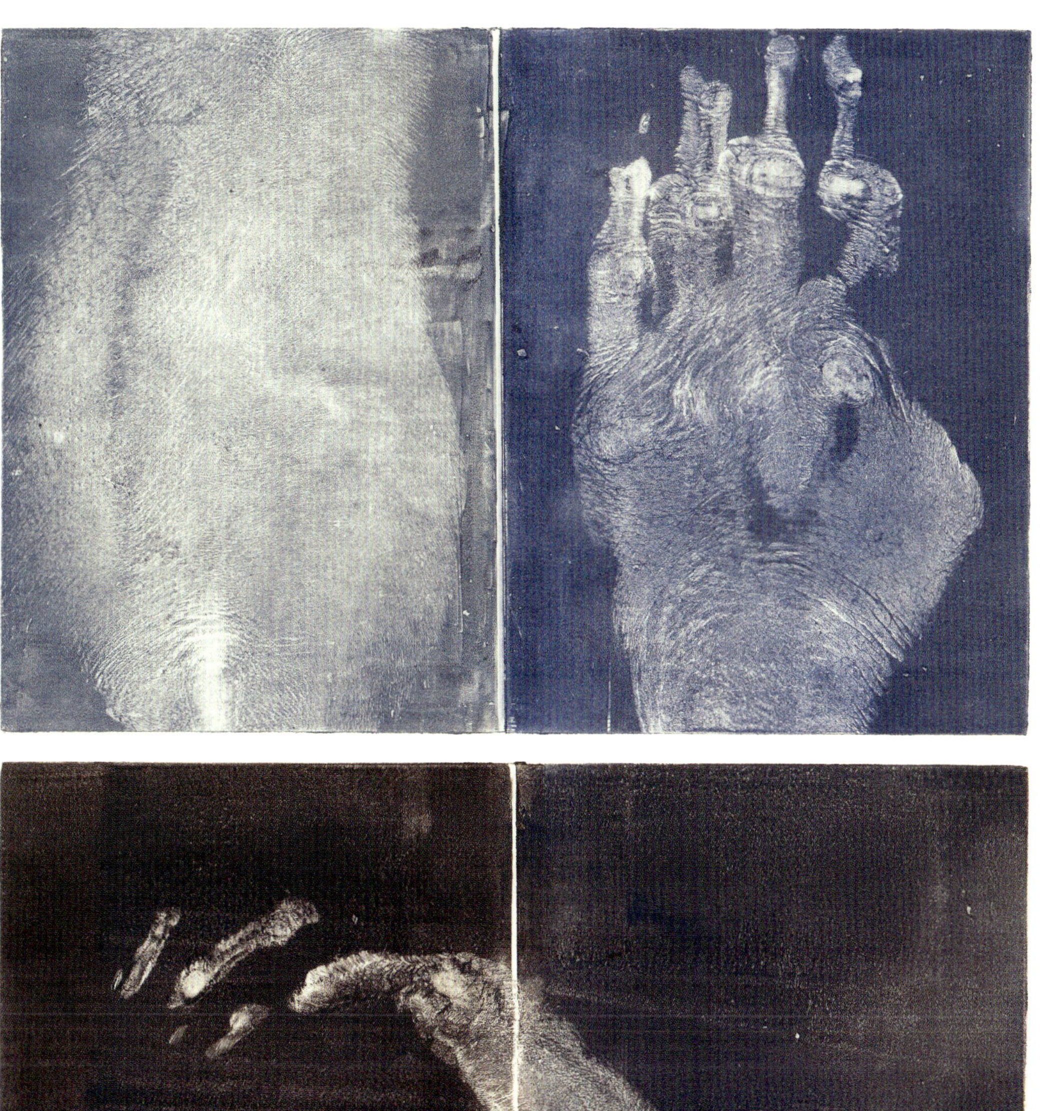

N.Y. 11 Sept 01 2001
Monotype
16 x 24.5cm

N.Y. 11 Sept 01 2001
Monotype
16 x 24.5cm

Collection: The artist

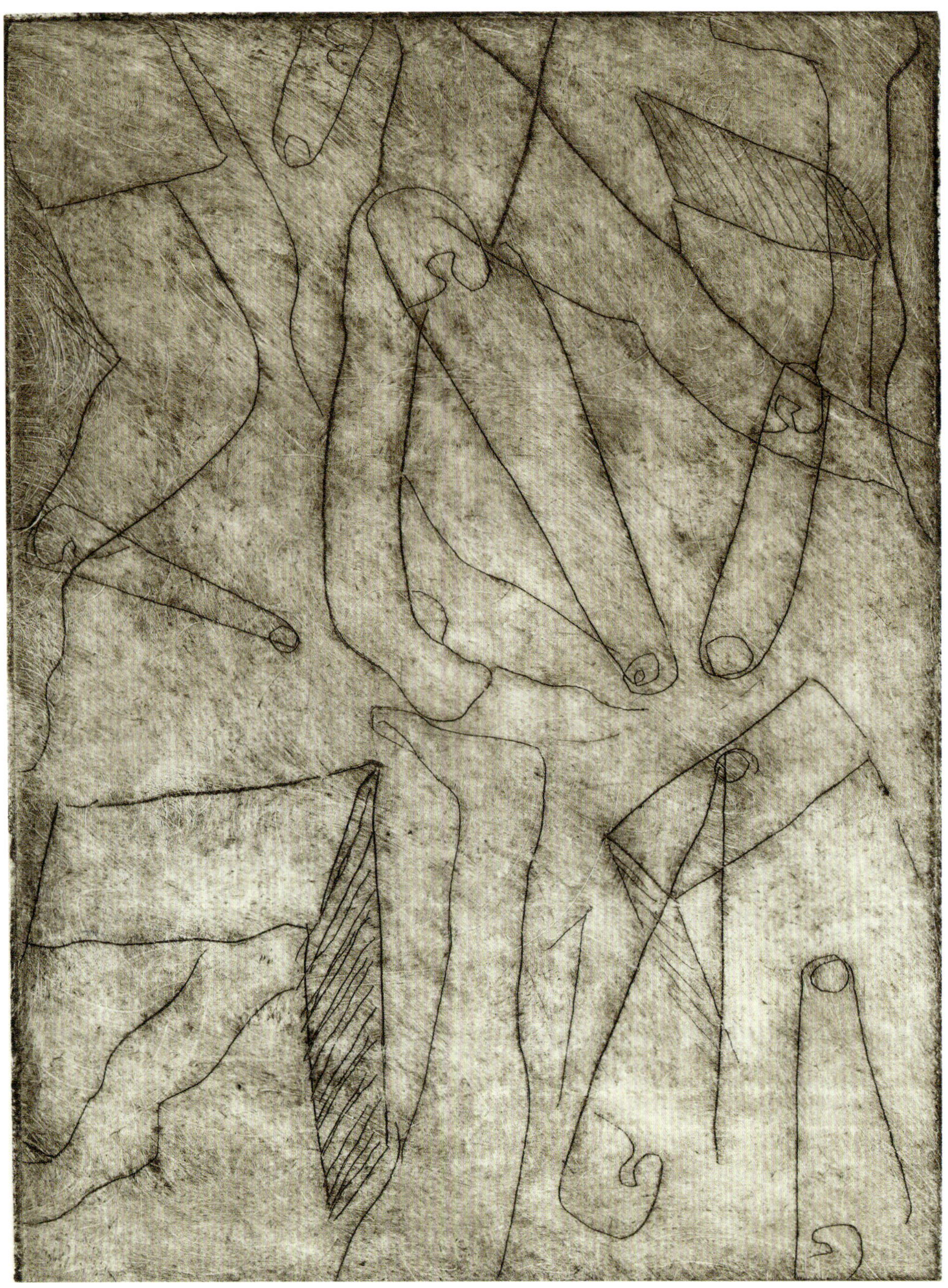

Safety pins and body parts c.2002
Etching
17 x 14cm
Collection: The artist

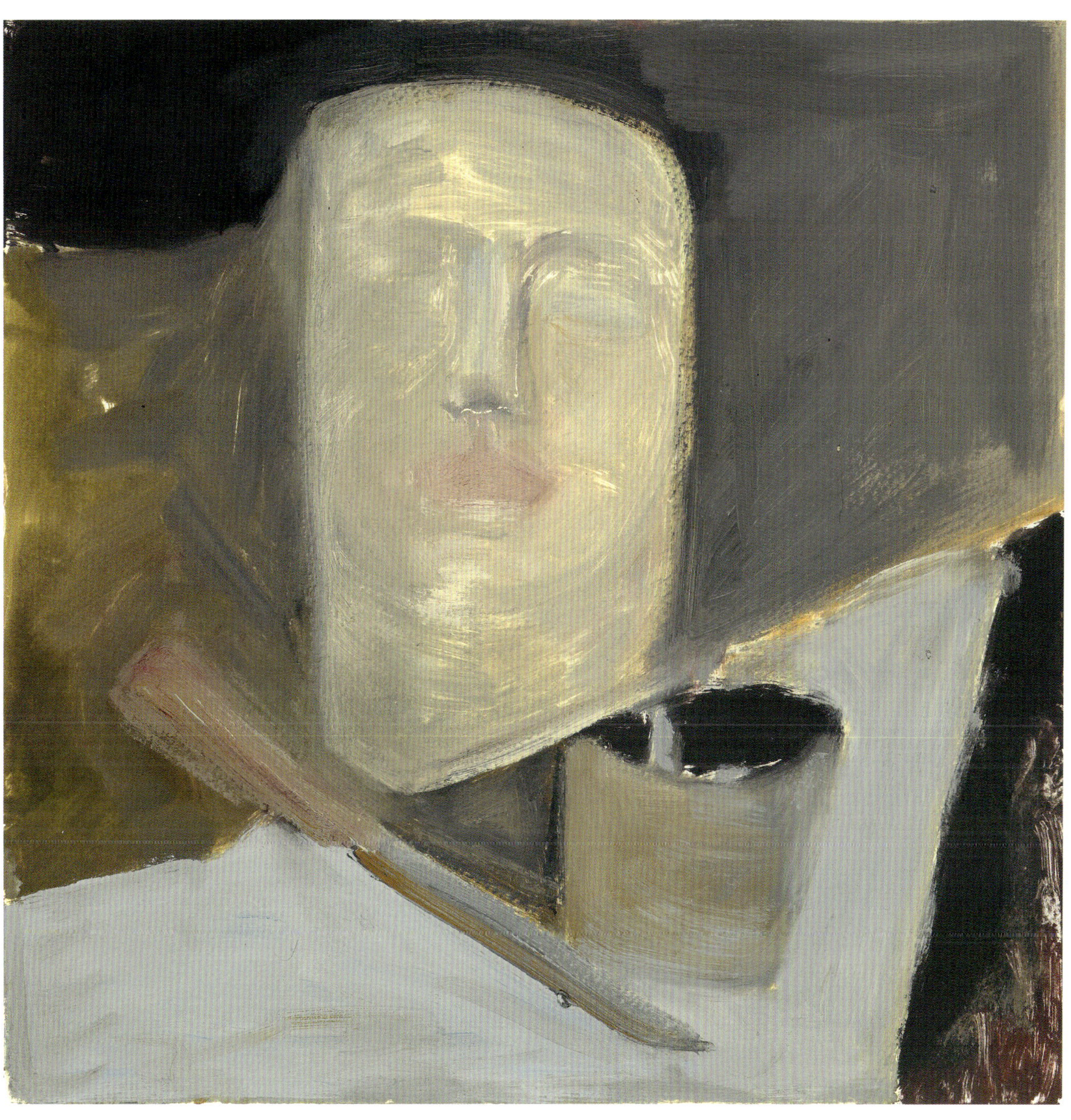

Mask with still life c.2005
Monotype
29 x 28cm
Collection: The artist

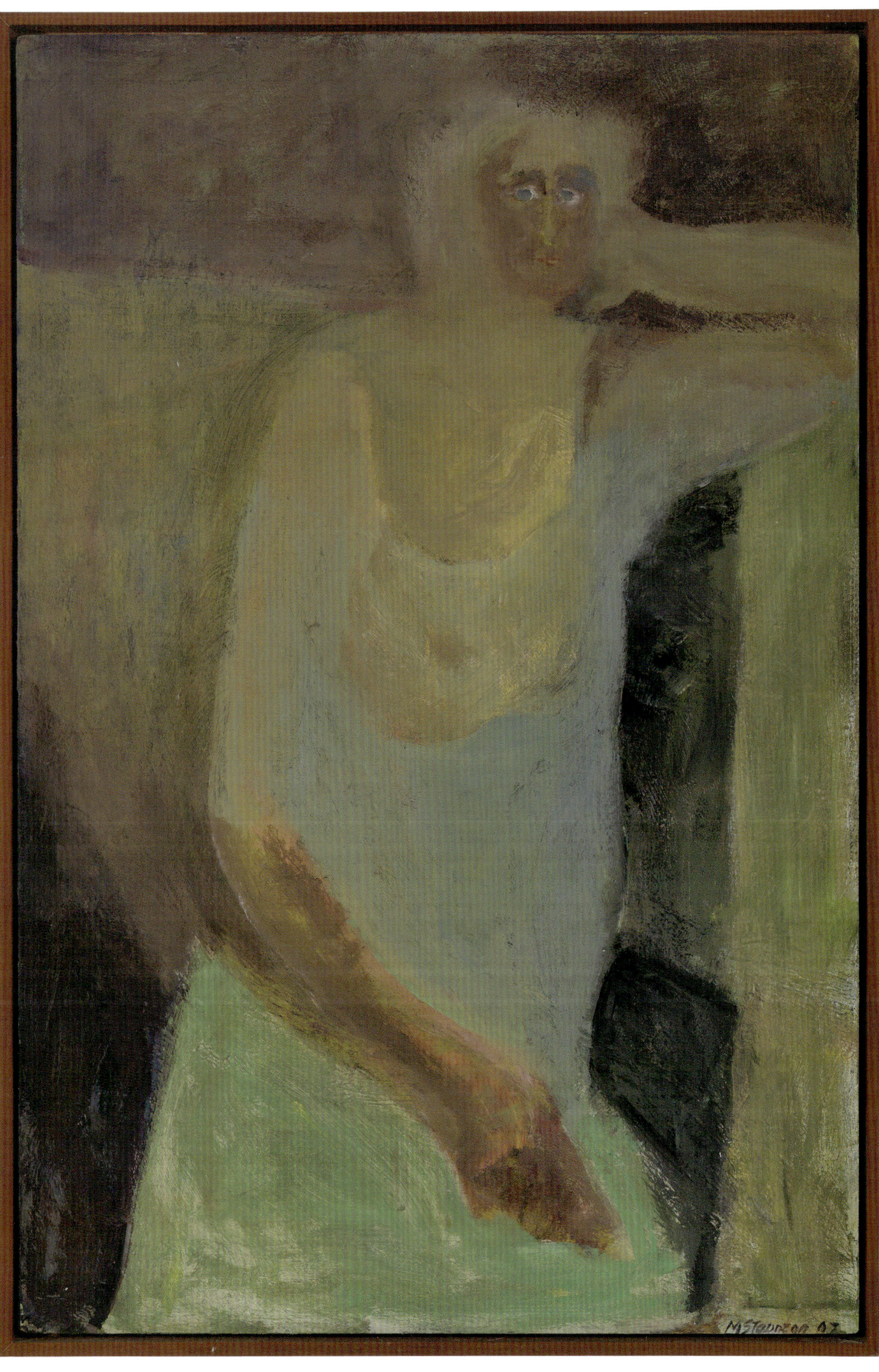

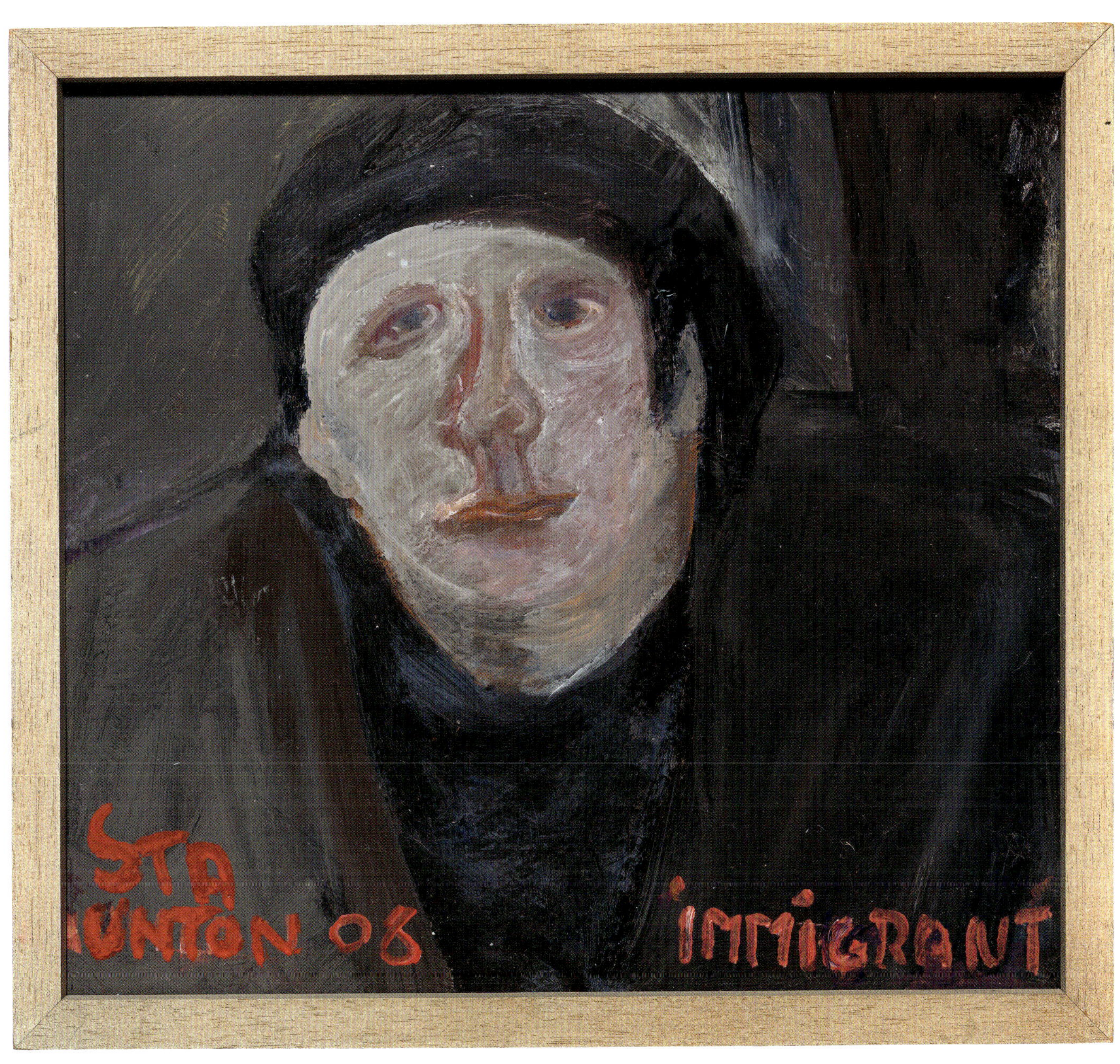

Reprise c.2007
Synthetic polymer paint on composition board
91.6 x 61.2cm; 95 x 64.3 x 6cm (framed)

Immigrant 2008
Synthetic polymer paint on card
23 x 26cm; 25.5 x 28.5 x 2.6cm (framed)

Collection: The artist

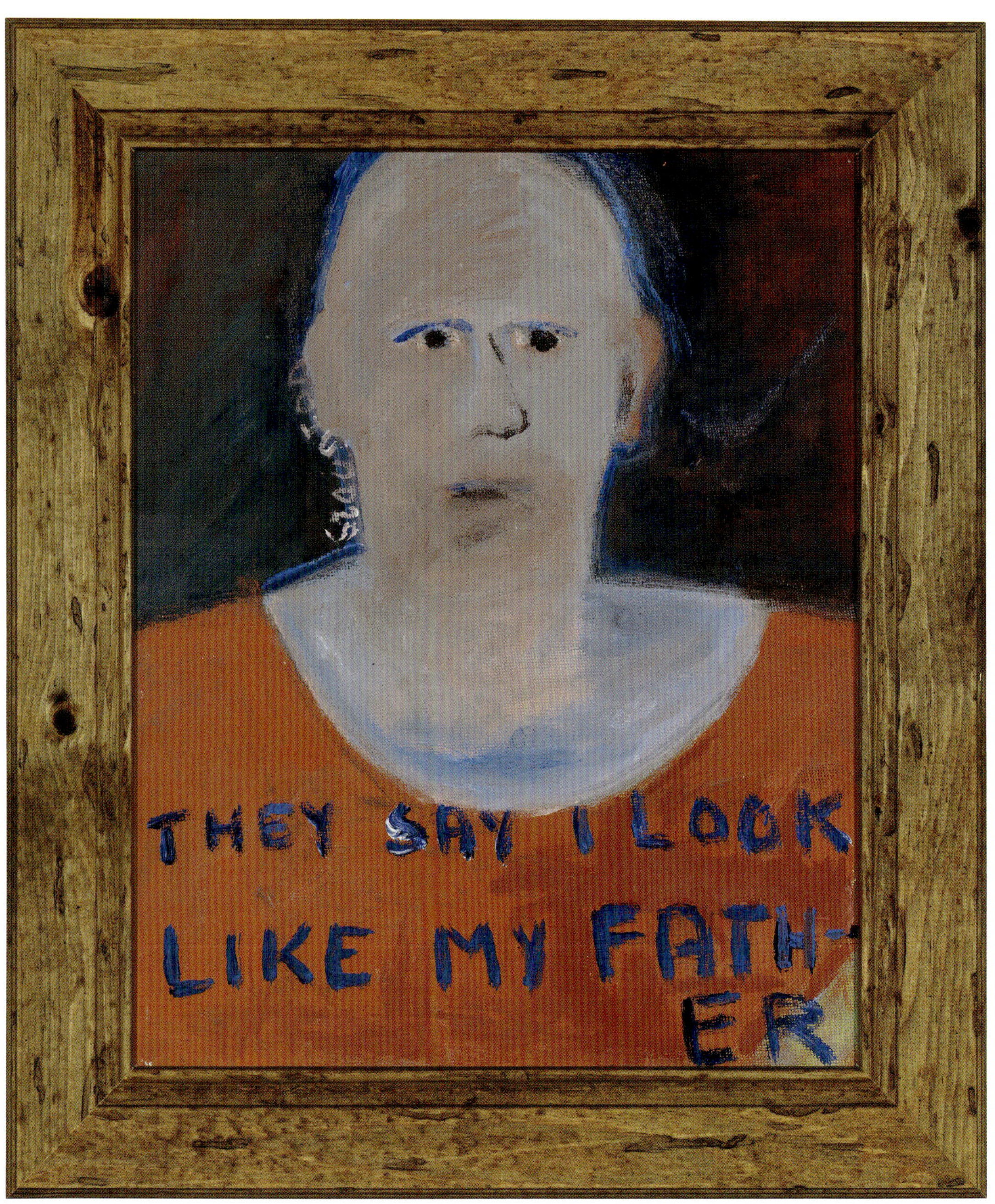

They say 2010
Synthetic polymer paint on canvas
29.5 x 24.4cm; 38 x 32.8 x 2.2cm (framed)
Purchased 2014 with funds from the Estate of Jessica Ellis through the Queensland Art Gallery | Gallery of Modern Art Foundation
Collection: Queensland Art Gallery

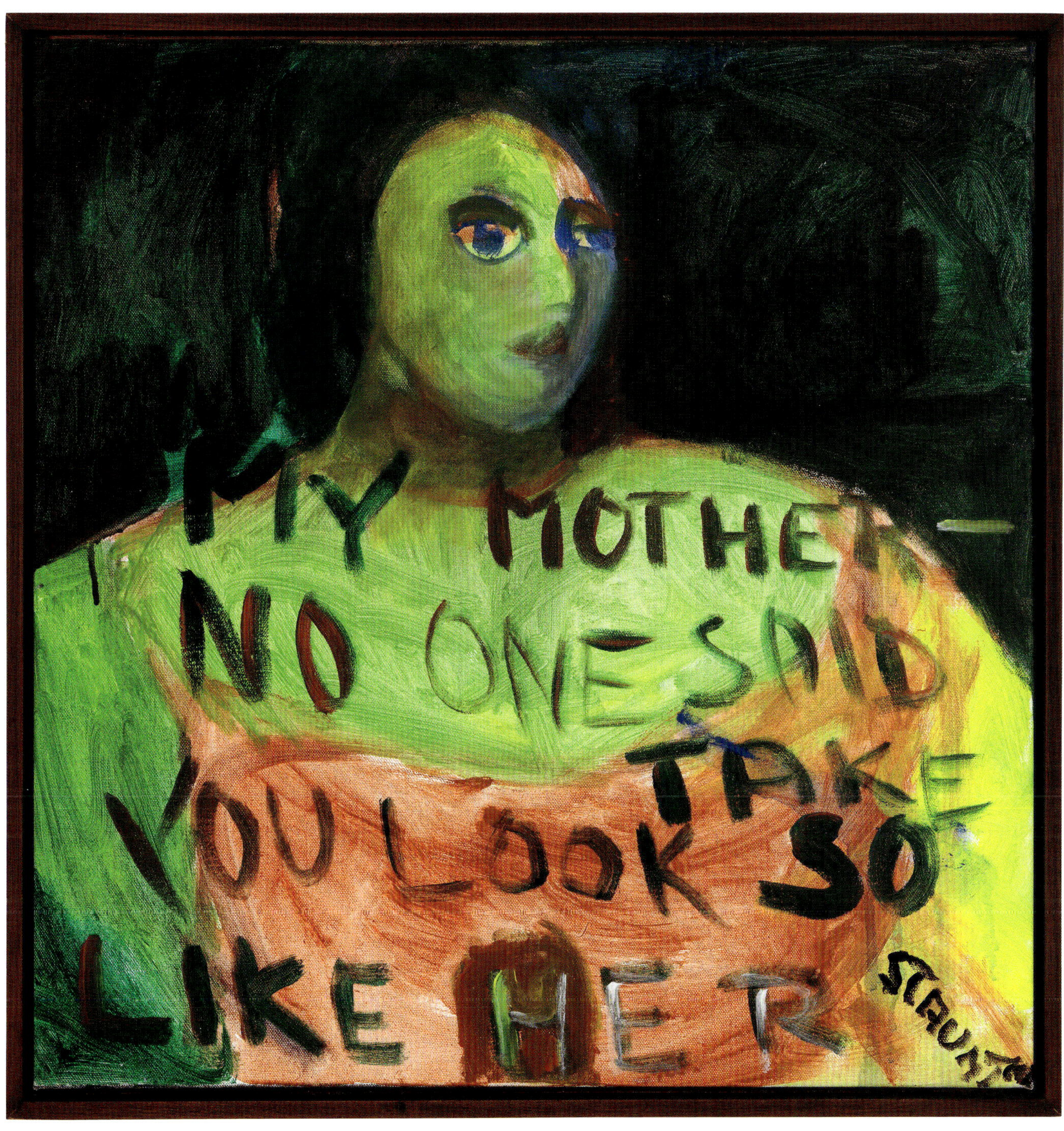

No one said 2010
Synthetic polymer paint on canvas
60.5 x 60cm; 64 x 63.4 x 5cm (framed)
Purchased 2014 with funds from the
Estate of Jessica Ellis through the
Queensland Art Gallery | Gallery of
Modern Art Foundation
Collection: Queensland Art Gallery

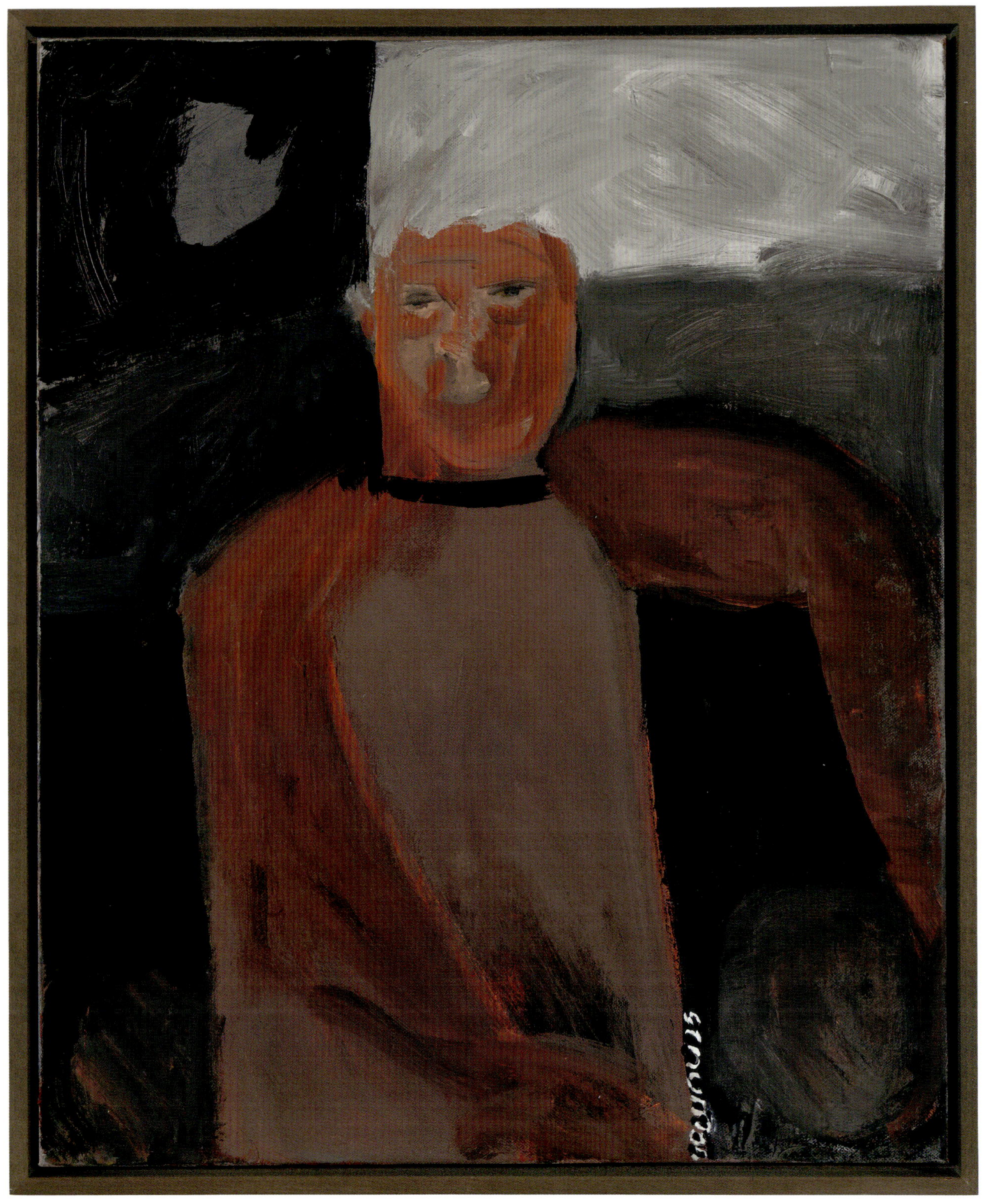

Game 2010
Synthetic polymer paint on canvas
61 x 50.7cm; 64 x 54 x 5cm (framed)
Collection: The artist

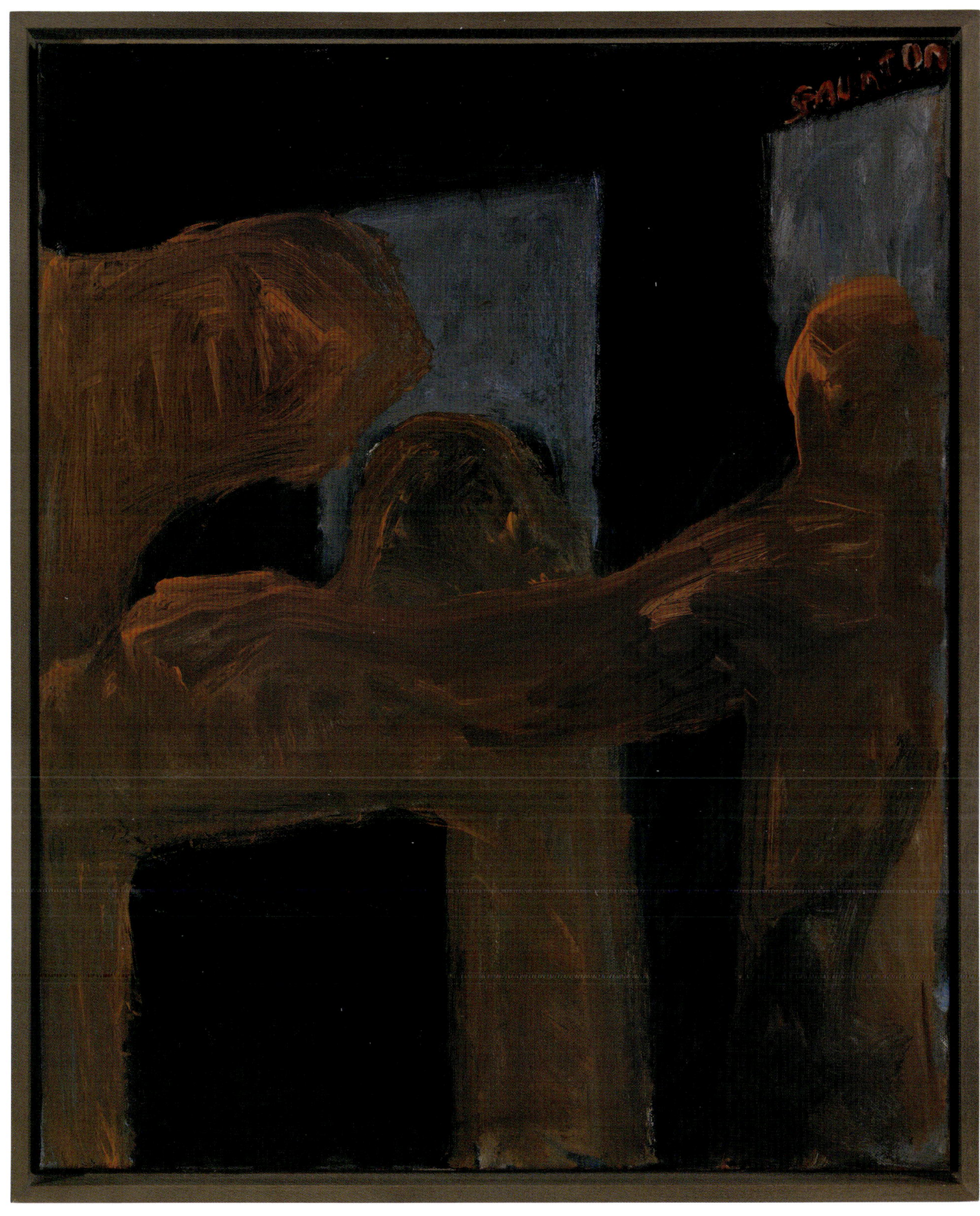

Men's business 2010
Synthetic polymer paint on canvas
60.8 x 50.7cm; 64.1 x 54 x 4.9cm (framed)
Collection: The artist

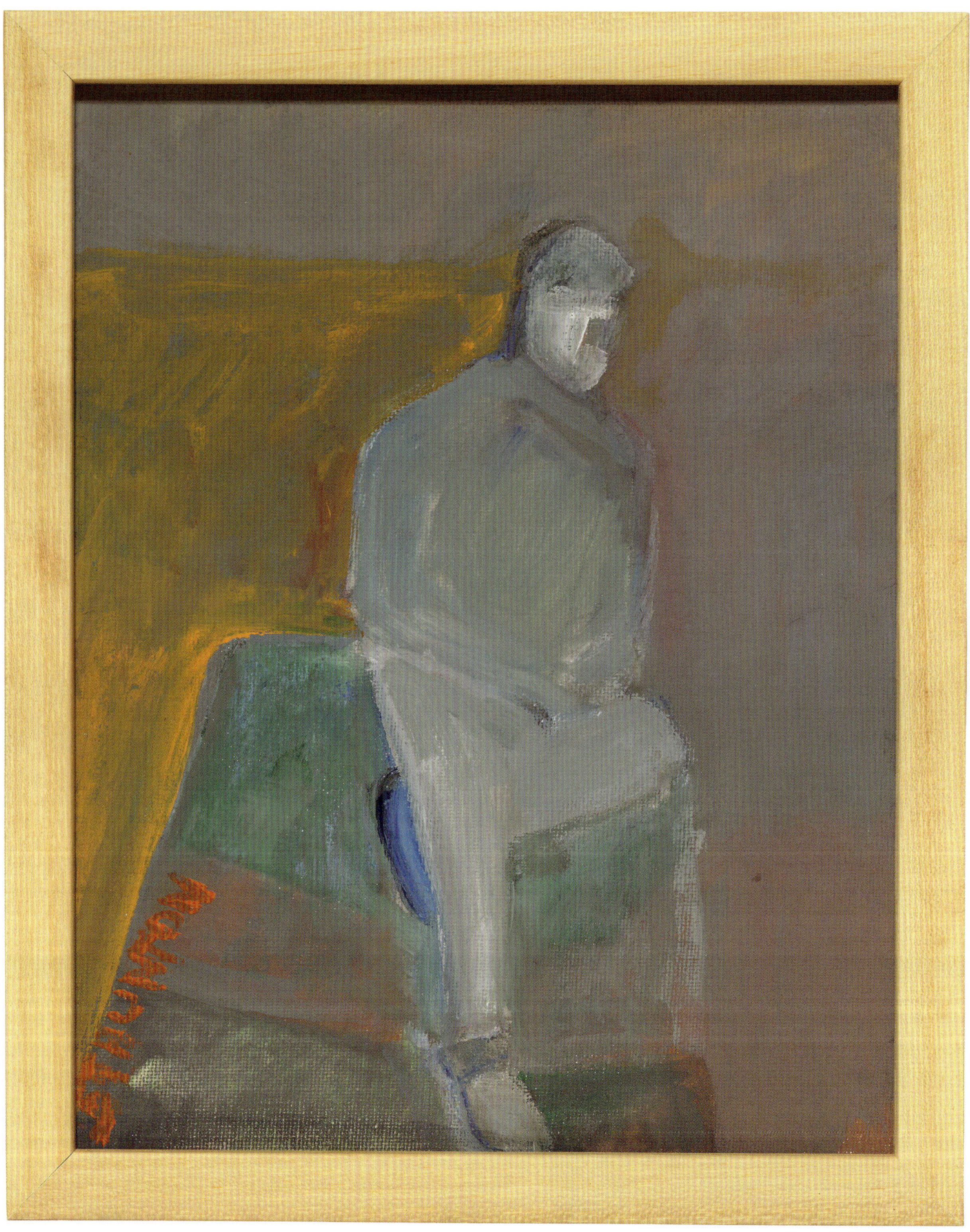

Solitary 2011
Gouache on canvas
25 x 20cm
Purchased 2011
Griffith University Art Collection

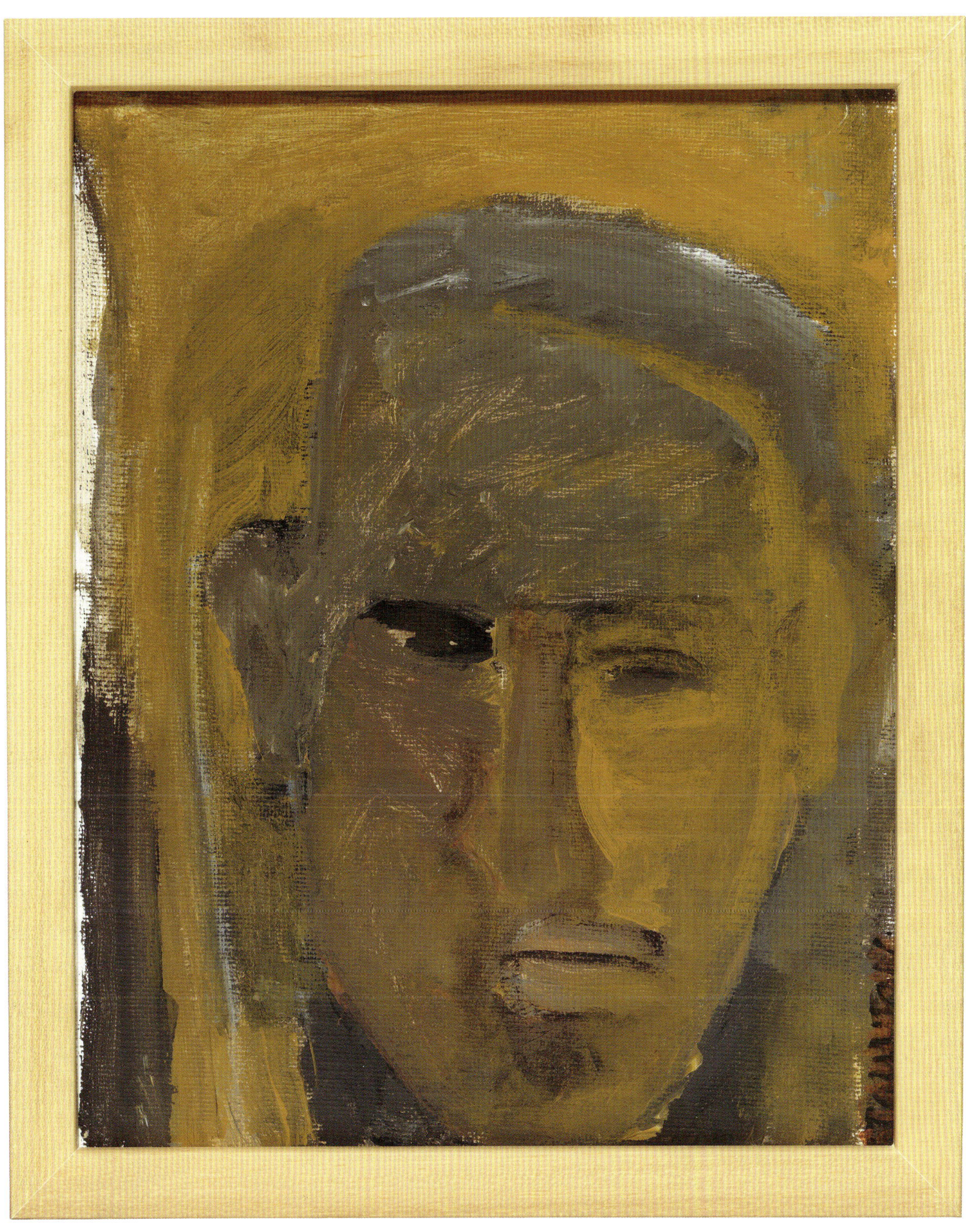

Apprentice 2011
Synthetic polymer paint on canvas
25 x 20cm
Purchased 2011
Griffith University Art Collection

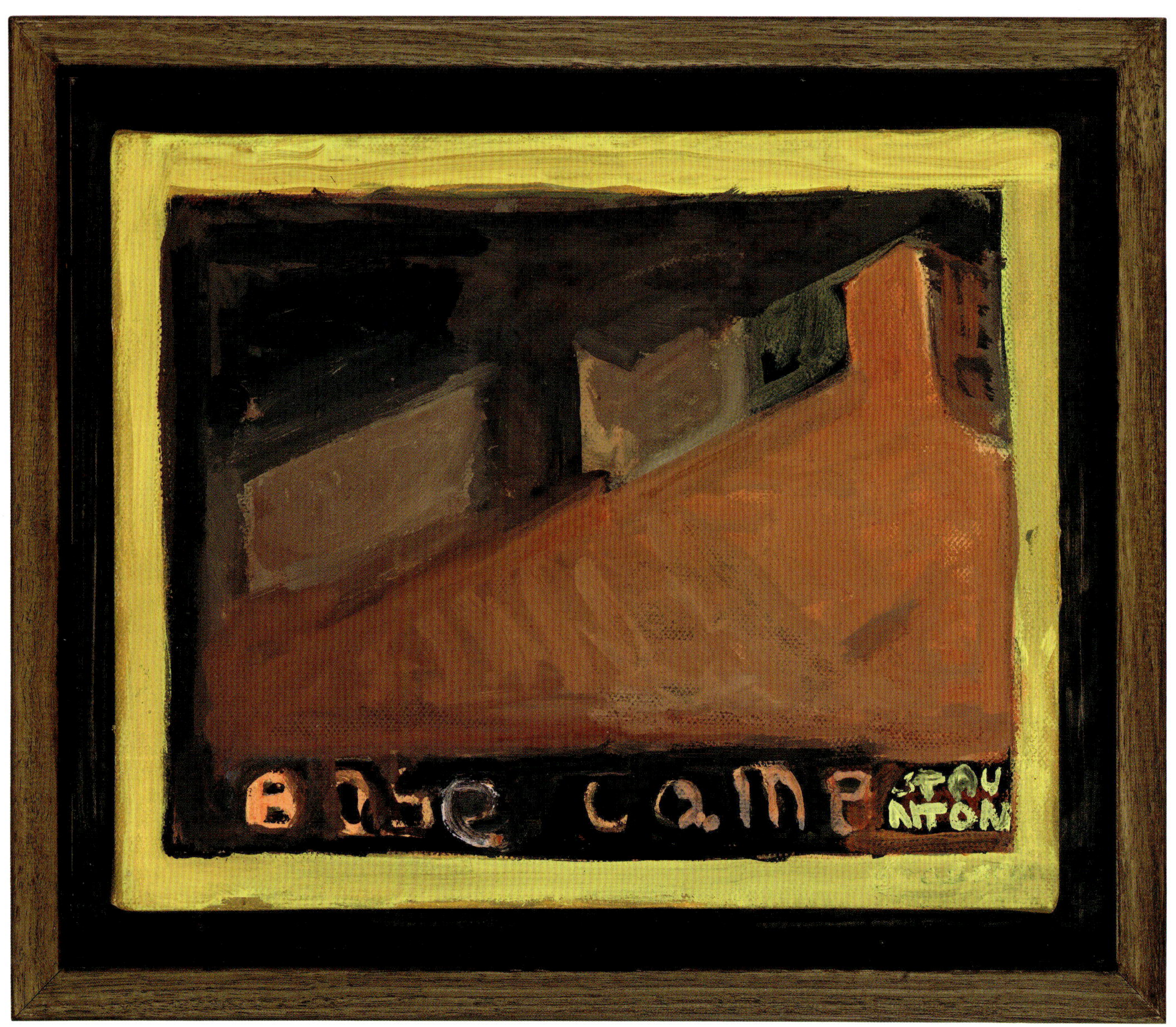

Base camp 2012
Synthetic polymer paint on canvas
20 x 25cm; 26.5 x 31.5 x 3.5cm (framed)
Collection: The artist

Amputee 2010
Synthetic polymer paint on canvas
25 x 20.5cm; 28.5 x 23.5 x 6cm (framed)
Private collection

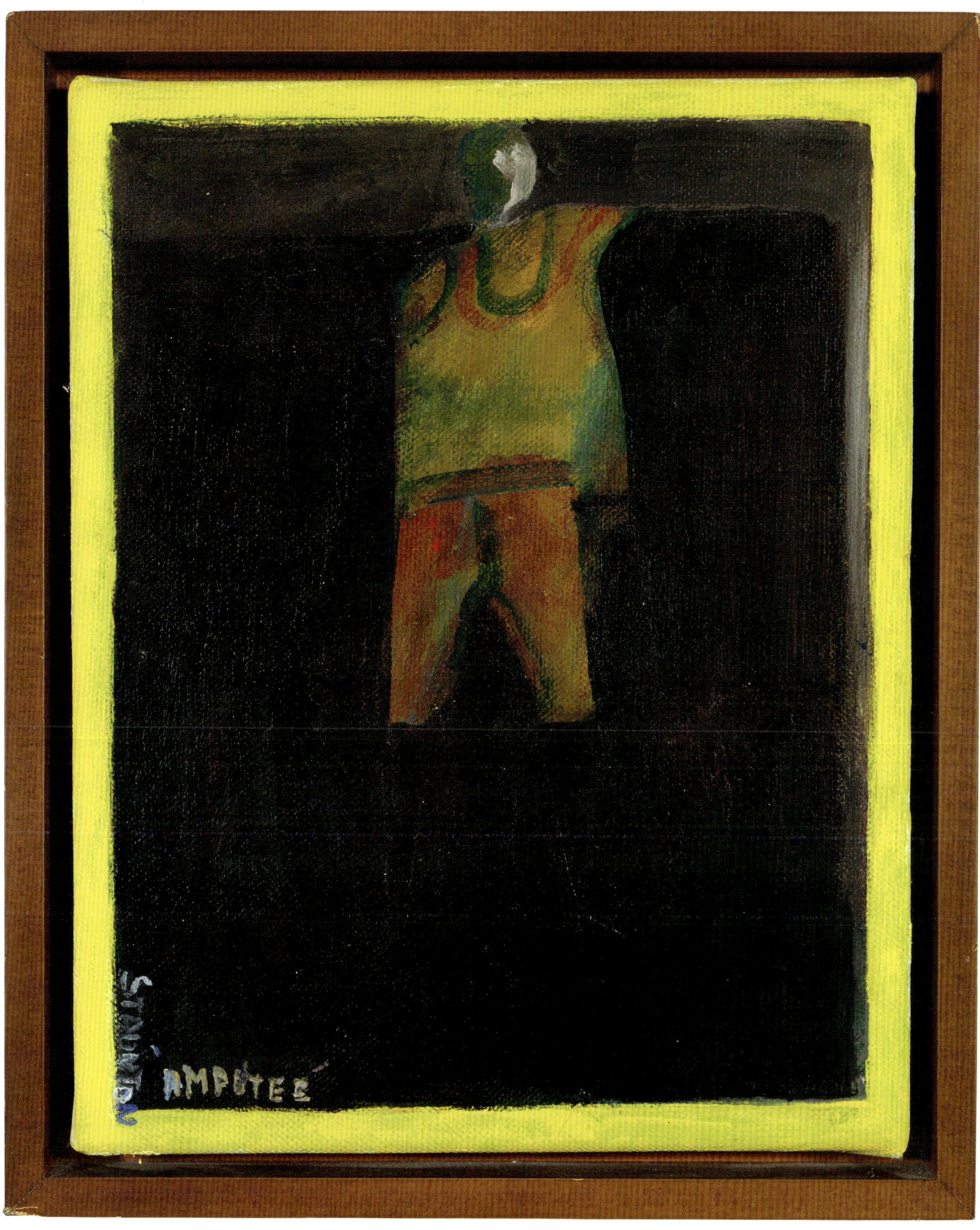
STAUNTON
AMPUTEE

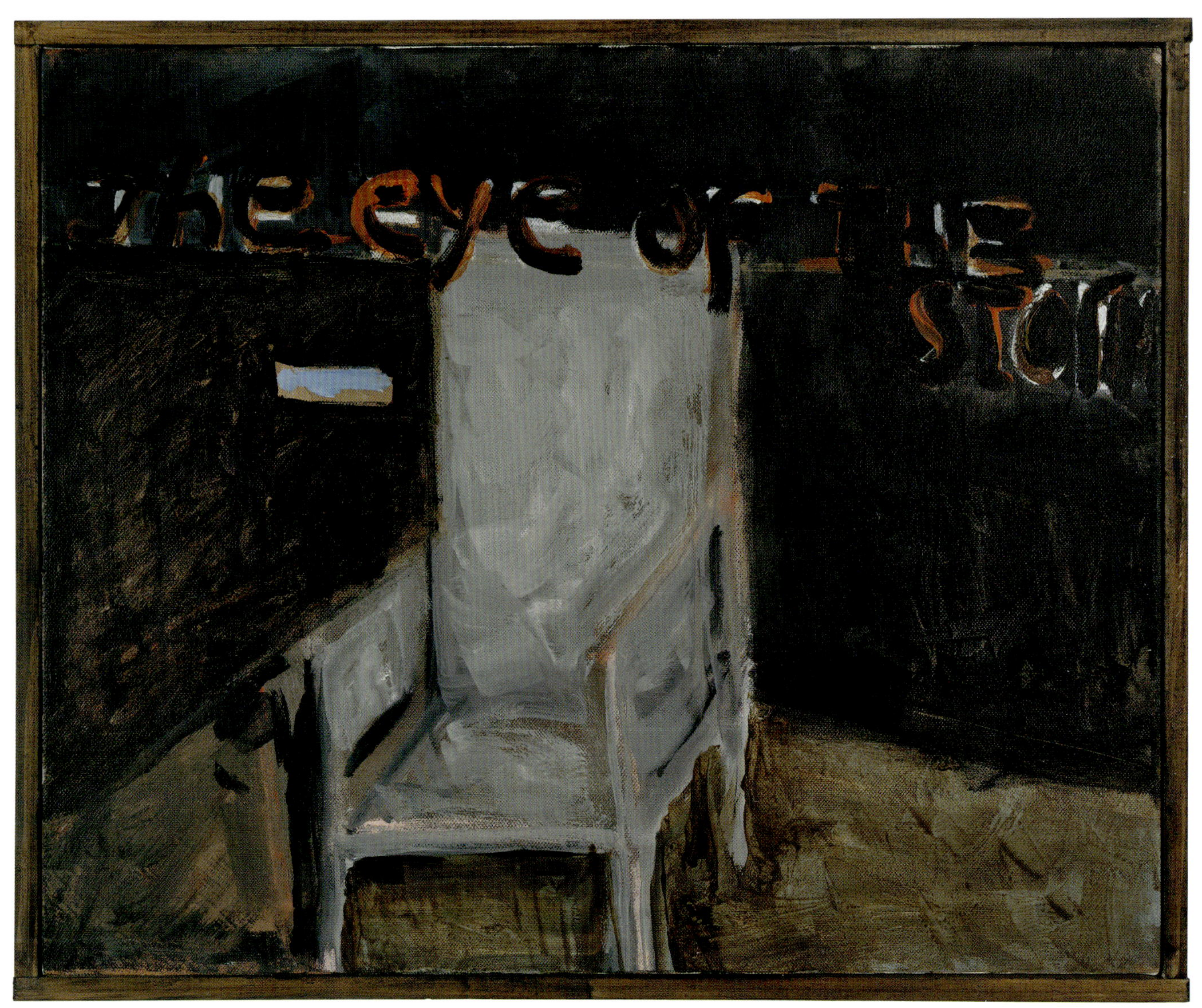

The eye of the storm 2012
Synthetic polymer paint on canvas
40.8 x 50.8cm; 43 x 53.2 x 4.5cm (framed)
Collection: The artist

The reader 2012
Synthetic polymer paint on canvas
76 x 61.2cm; 81 x 66.5 x 4.5cm (framed)
Syd Williams Collection

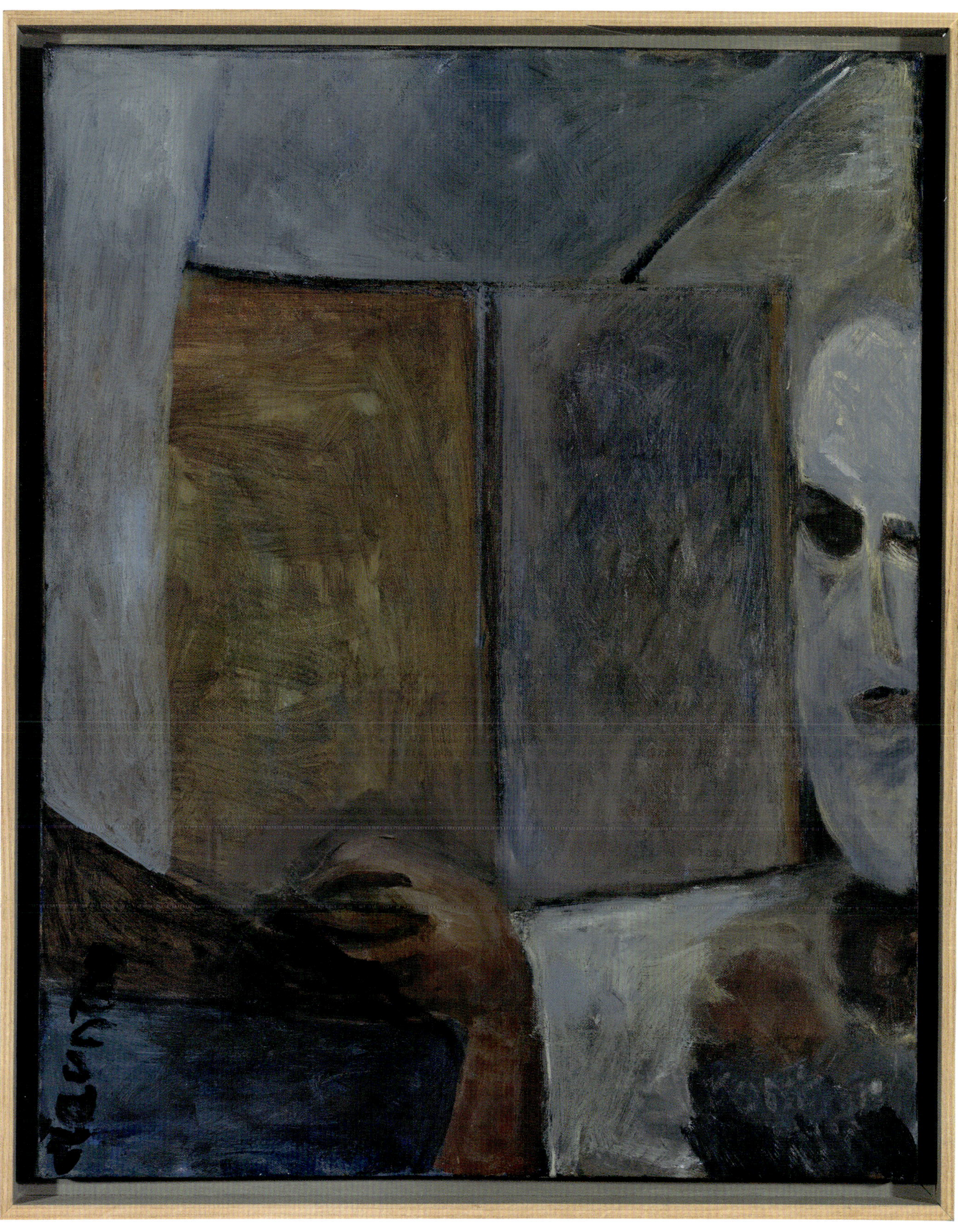

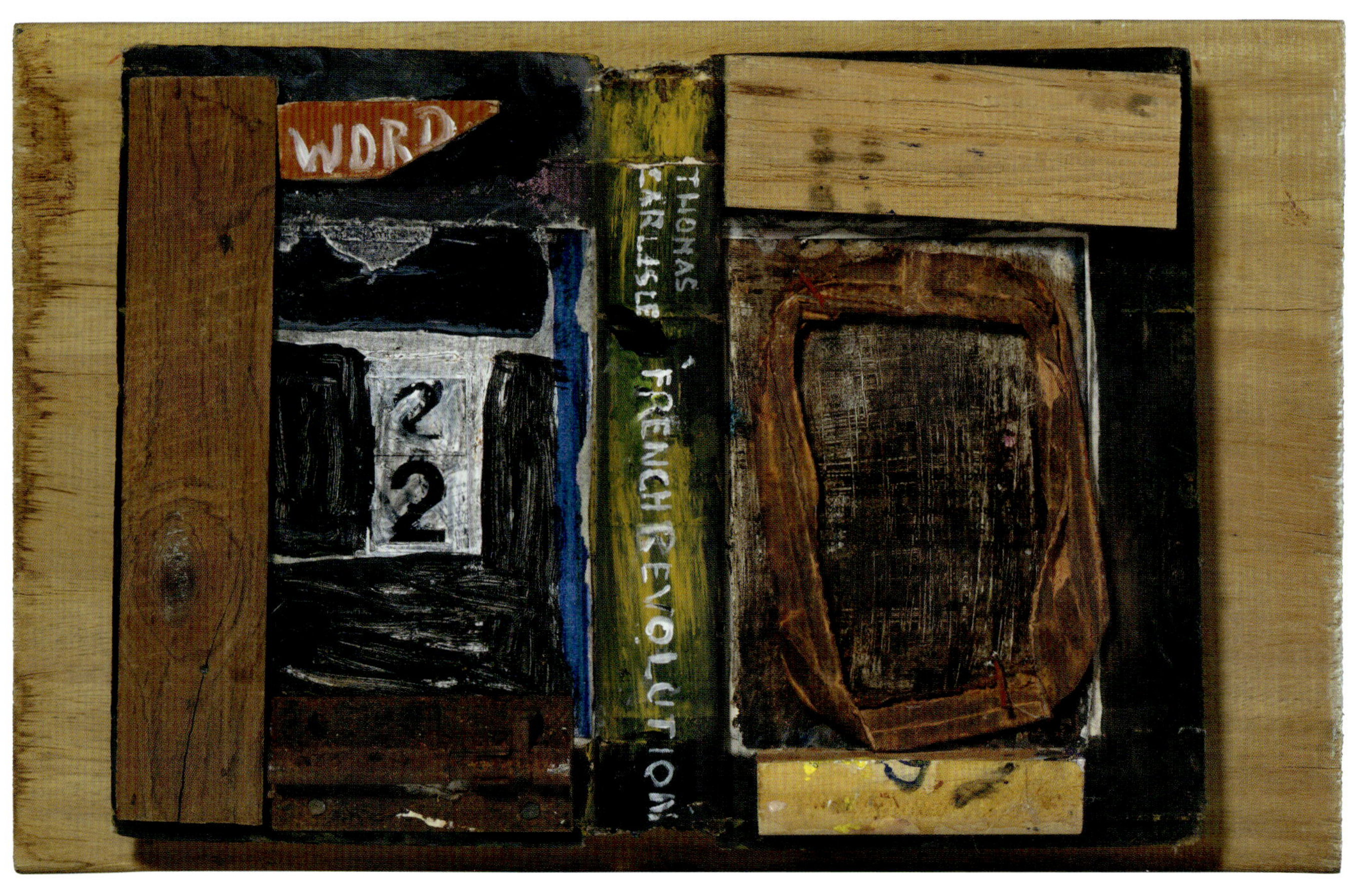

Word 2010
Wood, cloth-bound card, tin,
wire and synthetic polymer paint
21.2 x 34.4 x 7.8cm
Collection: University of Queensland, Brisbane
Gift of Michael Rayner, AM through the Australian Government's Cultural Gifts Program, 2014.

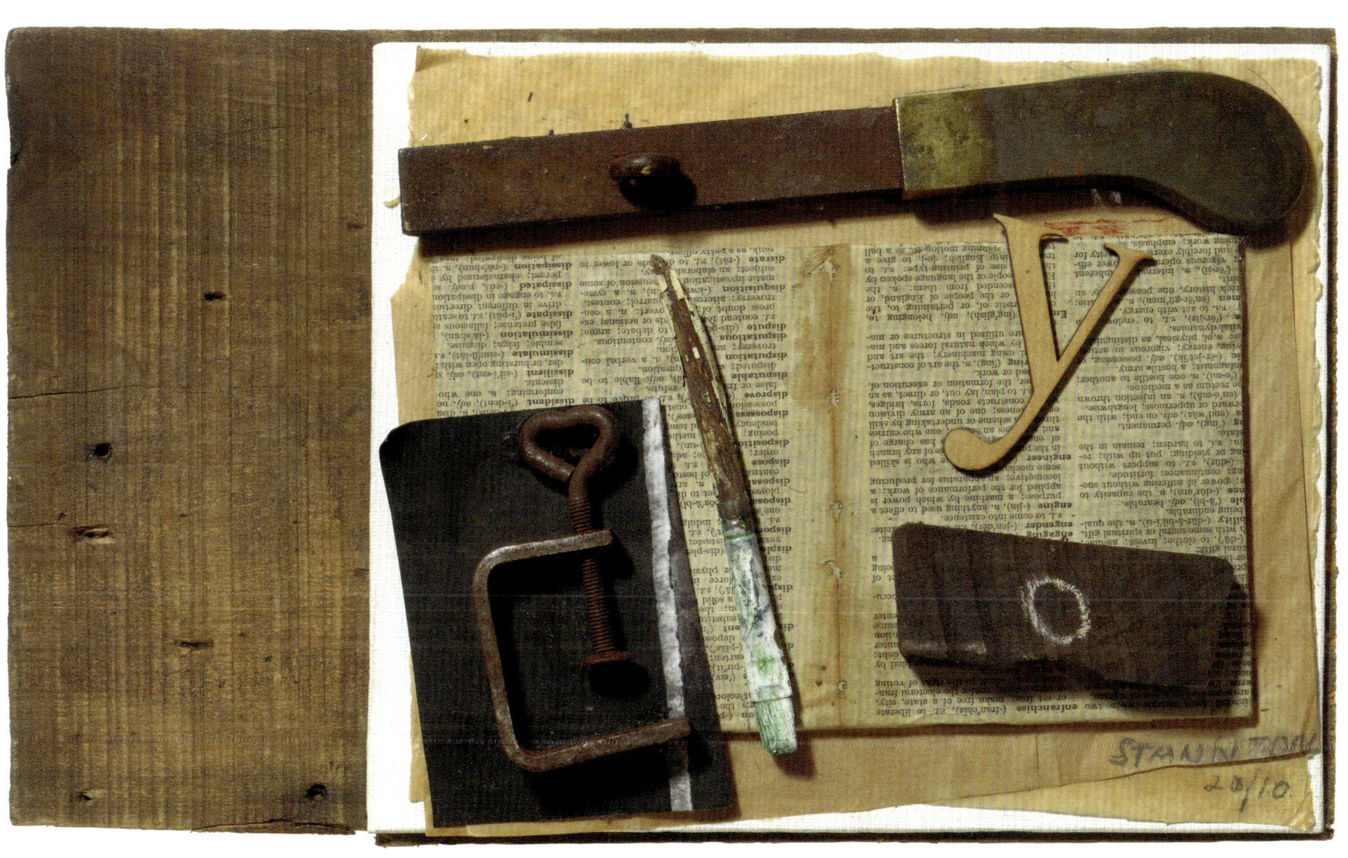

Yo 2010
Paper, metal, paint, ink, composition board, paintbrush and canvas board on wood
21 x 36 x 5cm
Private collection, Brisbane

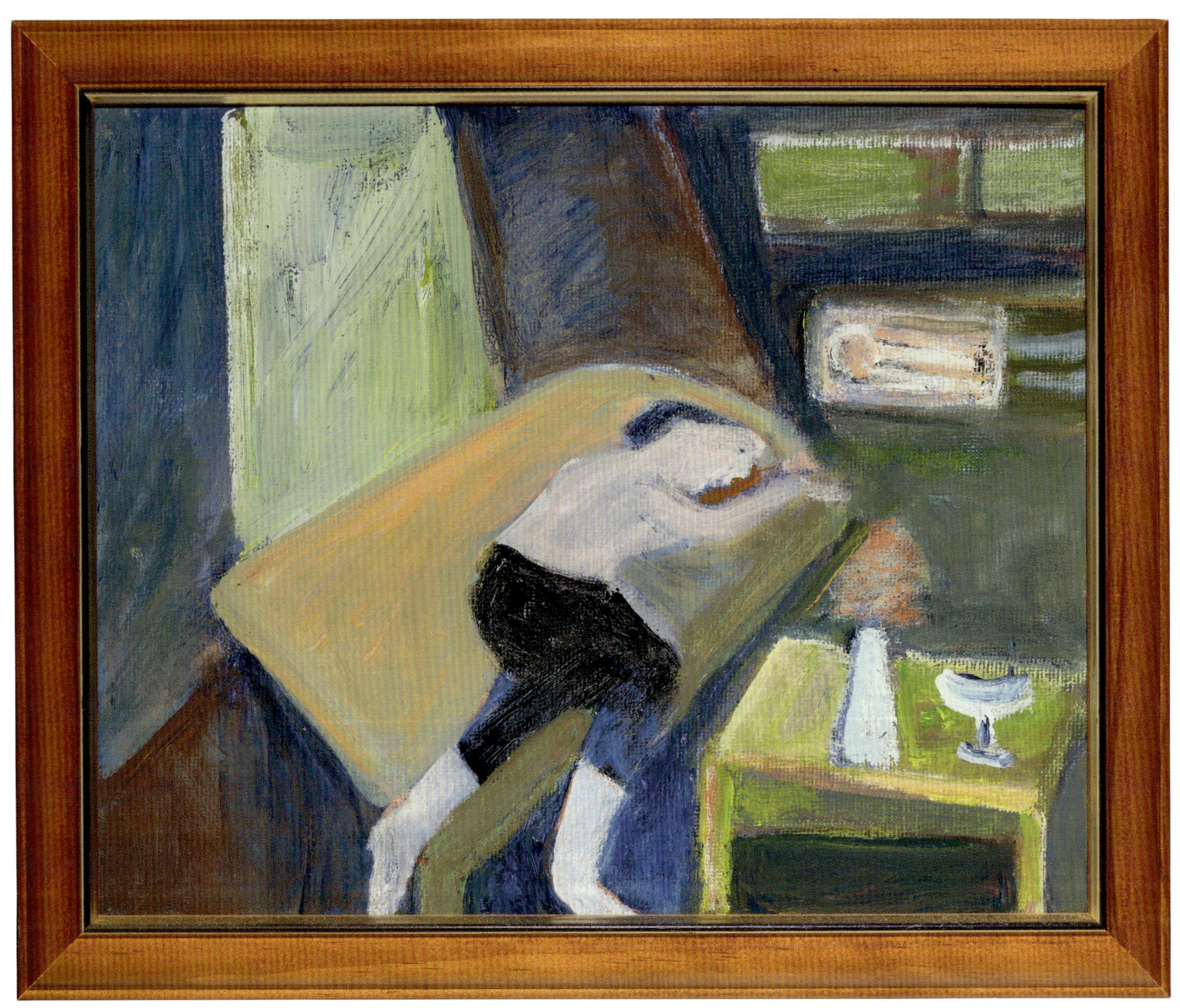

Flake 2012
Synthetic polymer paint on canvas
19.5 x 24.3cm; 23.5 x 28.5 x 2.7cm (framed)
Private collection, Brisbane

Postcard for Emily Dickinson 2012
Synthetic polymer paint on canvas
16.9 x 11.9cm; 23.2 x 18.2 x 2.5cm (framed)
Private collection, Los Angeles

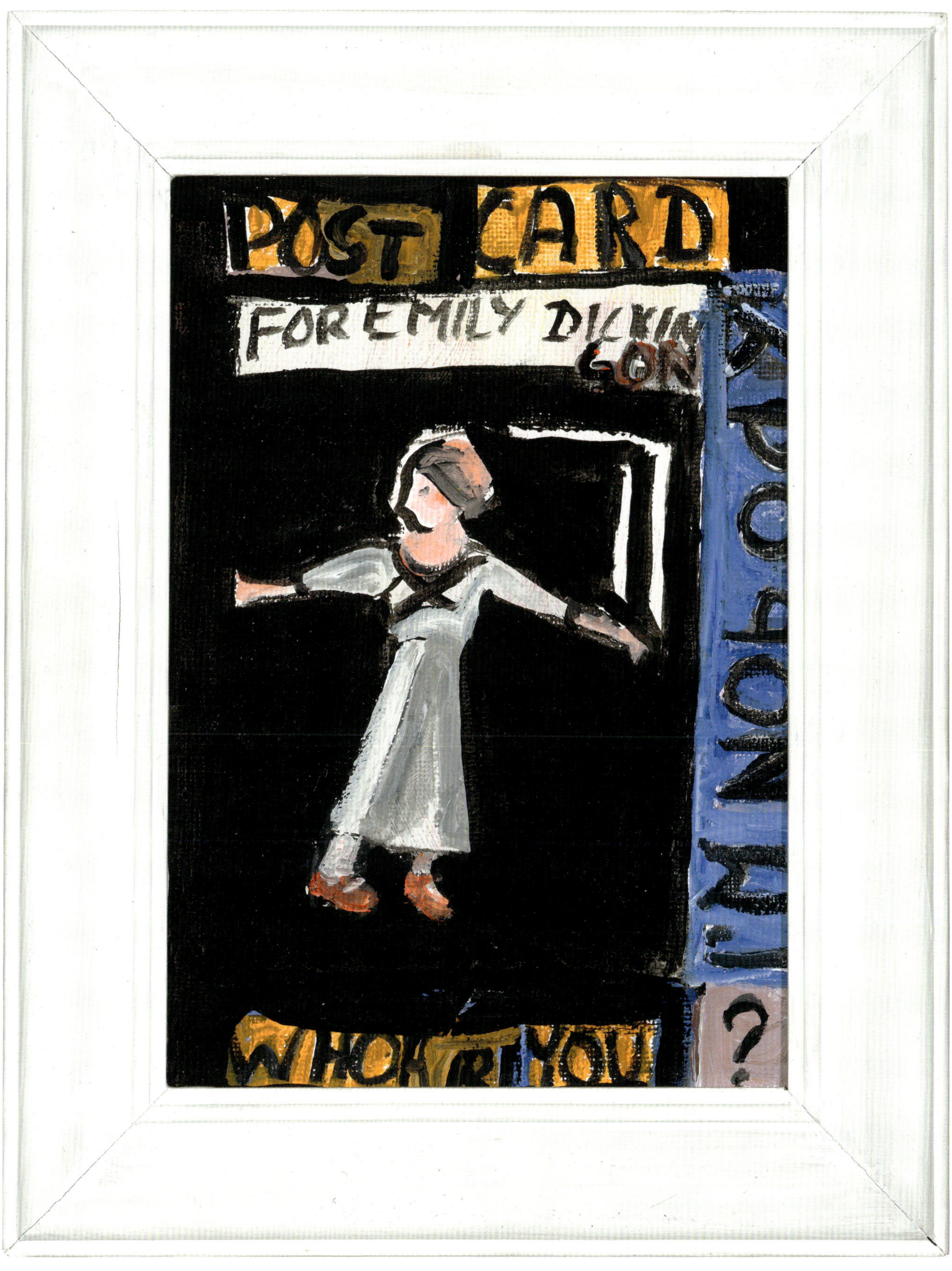
POST CARD
FOR EMILY DICKIN
SON
I'M NOBODY
WHO ART YOU
?

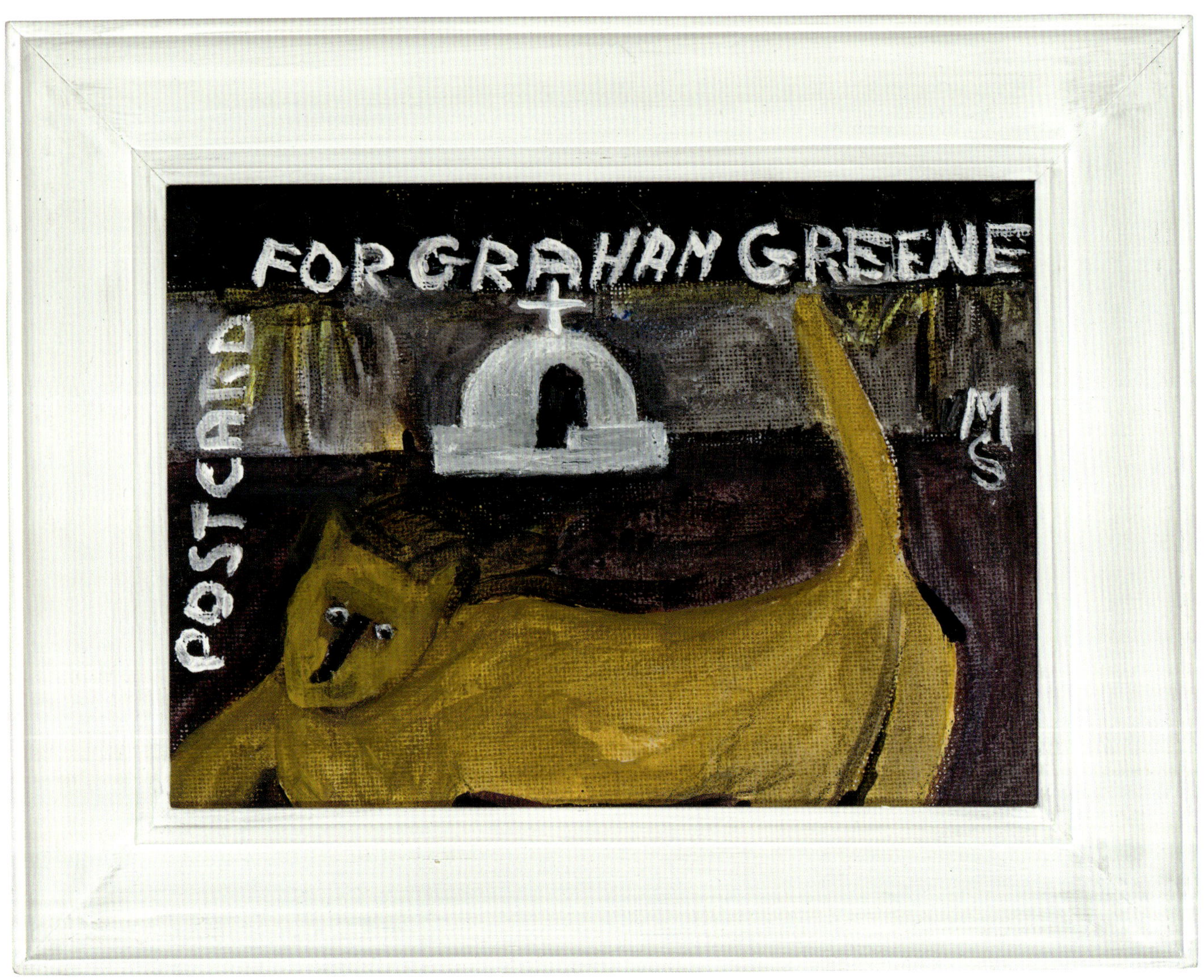

Postcard for Graham Greene 2012
Synthetic polymer paint on canvas board
11.8 x 17cm; 18 x 23.2 x 1.4cm (framed)
Private collection

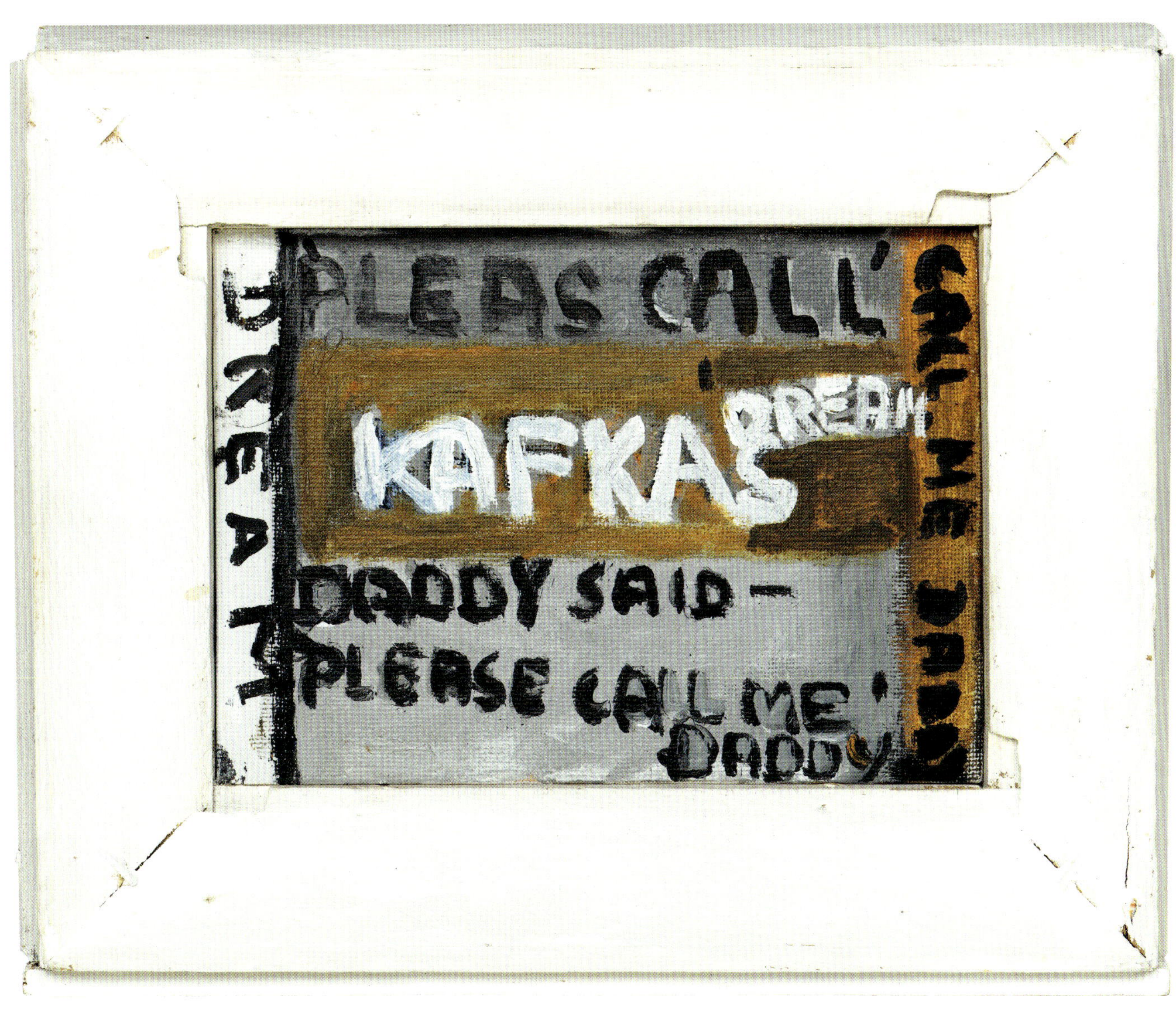

Postcard for Kafka 2012
Synthetic polymer paint on canvas board
12.5 x 17.6cm; 21.5 x 27.5 x 4.5cm (framed)
Collection: Dr Morris Low, Brisbane

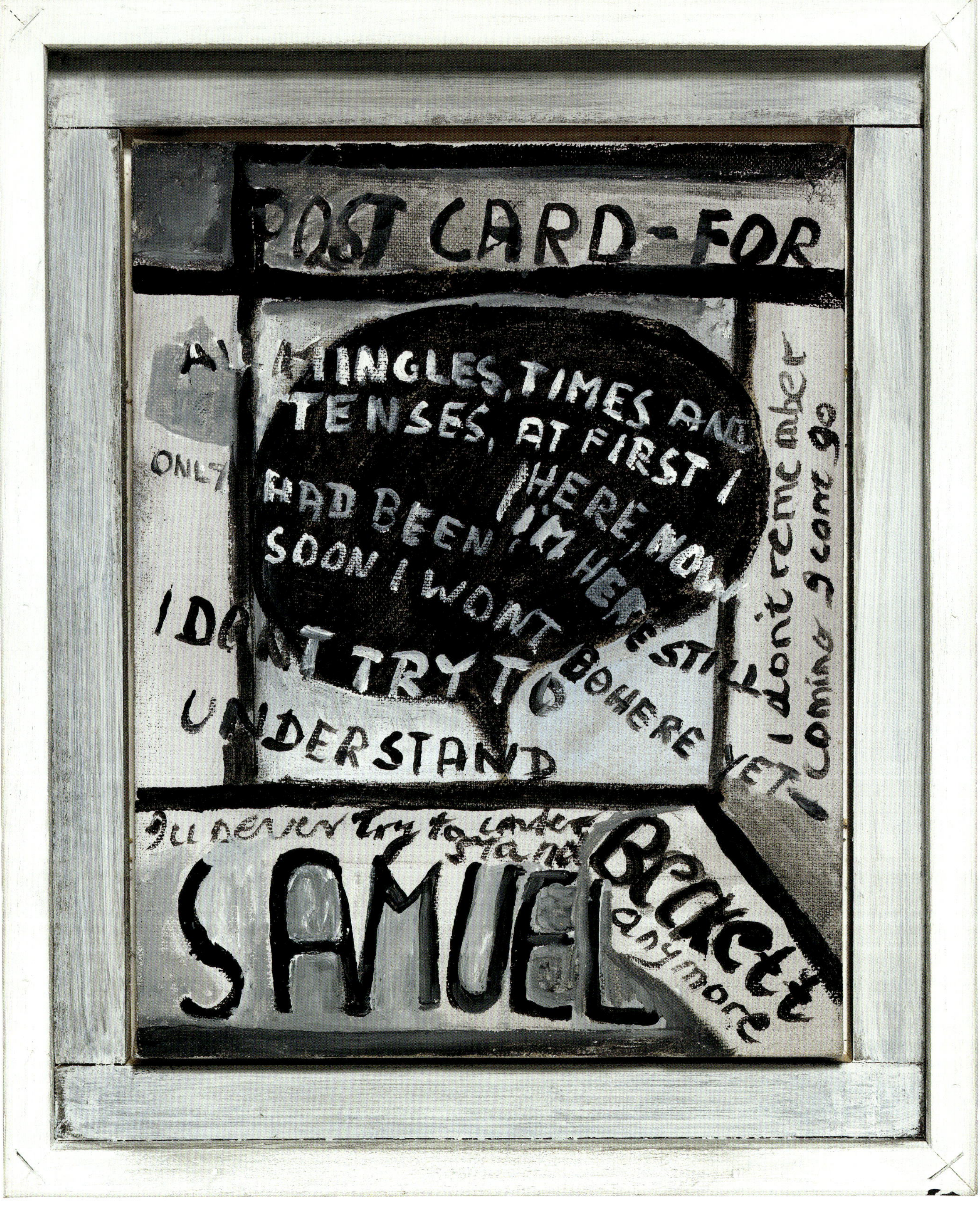
POST CARD-FOR
MINGLES, TIMES AND
TENSES, AT FIRST I
ONLY
HERE, NOW
HAD BEEN, I'M HERE
SOON I WONT BE HERE STILL
I DONT TRY TO
UNDERSTAND
BE HERE YET
i dont remember
coming i cant go
SAMUEL
Beckett
anymore

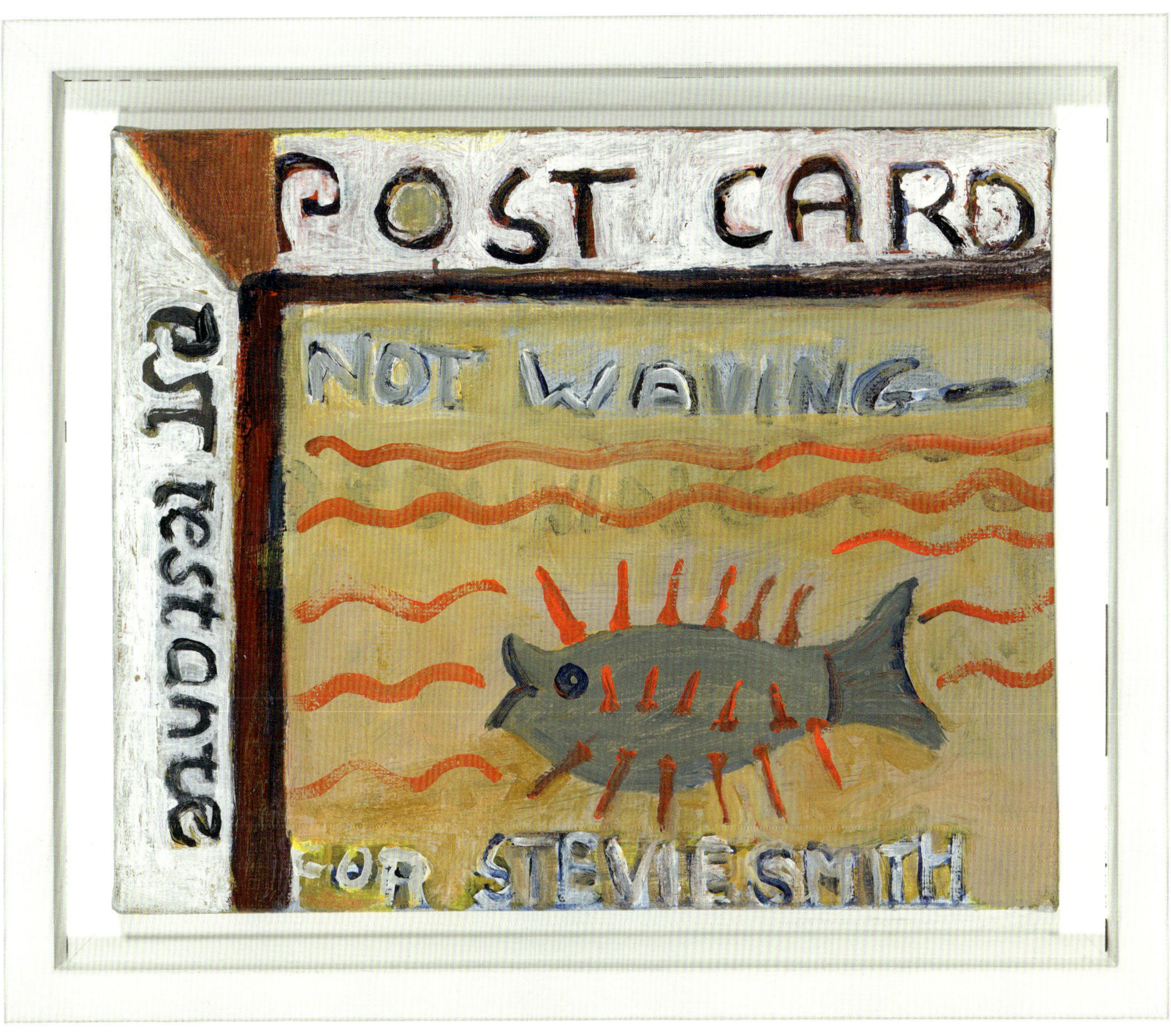

Postcard for Samuel Beckett 2012
Synthetic polymer paint on canvas
25 x 20.5cm; 33 x 28 x 5.5cm (framed)
The Paul Eliadis Collection of
Contemporary Art, Brisbane

Postcard for Stevie Smith 2012
Synthetic polymer paint on canvas
20.4 x 25.4cm; 26 x 31.2 x 3.7cm (framed)
Collection: The artist

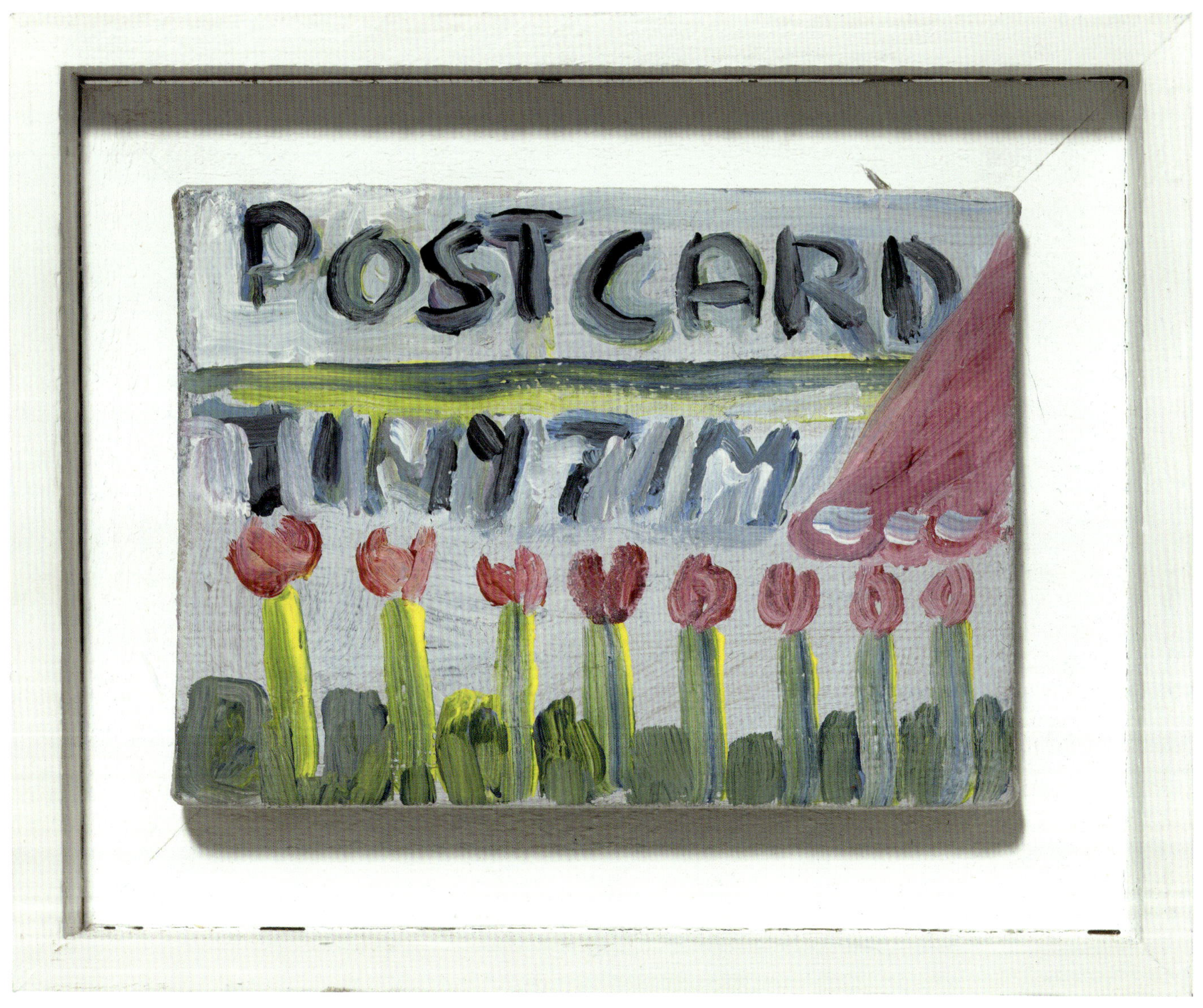

Postcard for Tiny Tim 2012
Synthetic polymer paint on canvas
8.2 x 11.8cm; 13 x 16.4 x 2.5cm (framed)
Private collection, Brisbane

Profile no.1 2012
Synthetic polymer paint on canvas
30.5 x 25cm; 36 x 30.8 x 5cm (framed)
Collection: Gino Milani, Brisbane

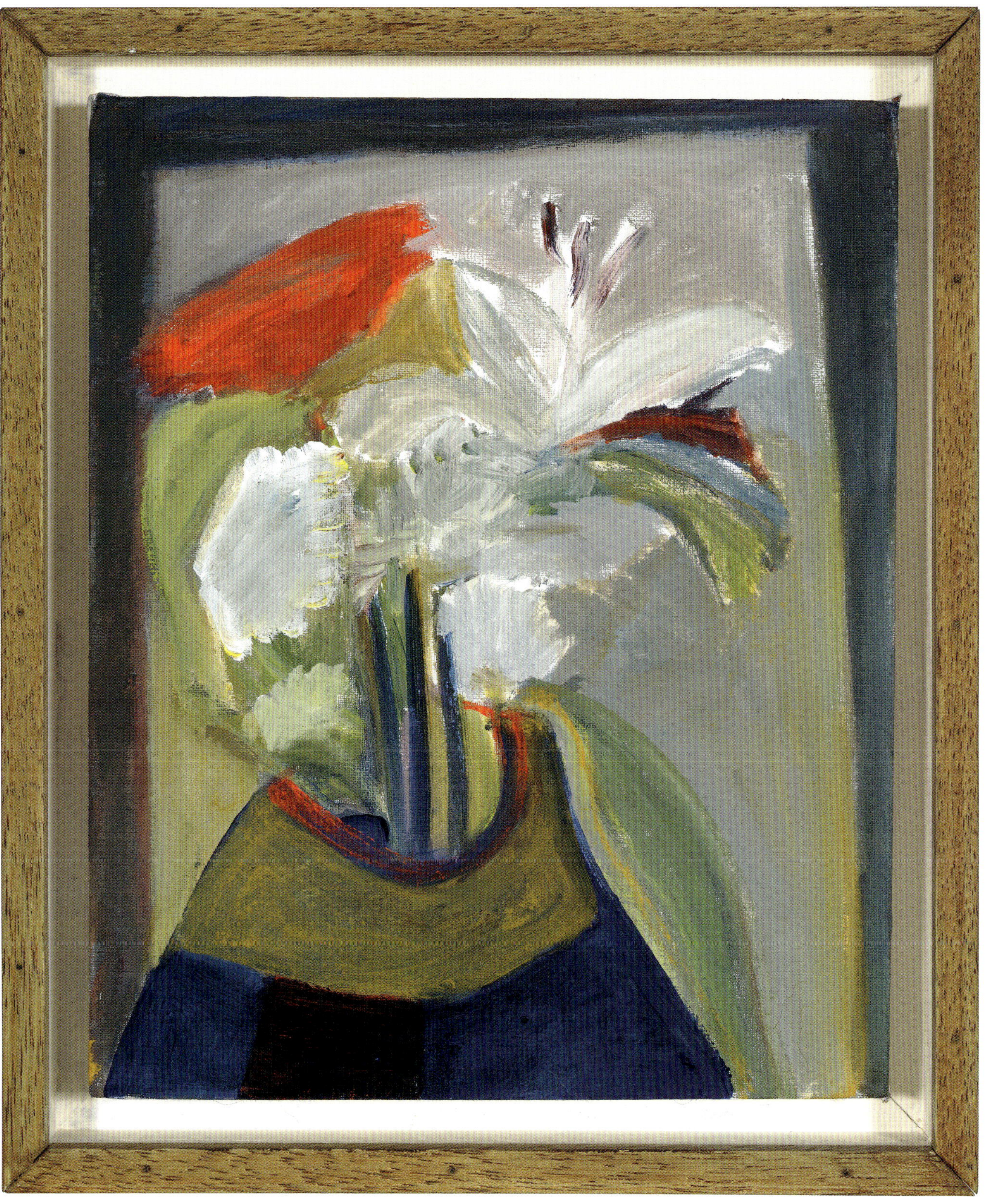

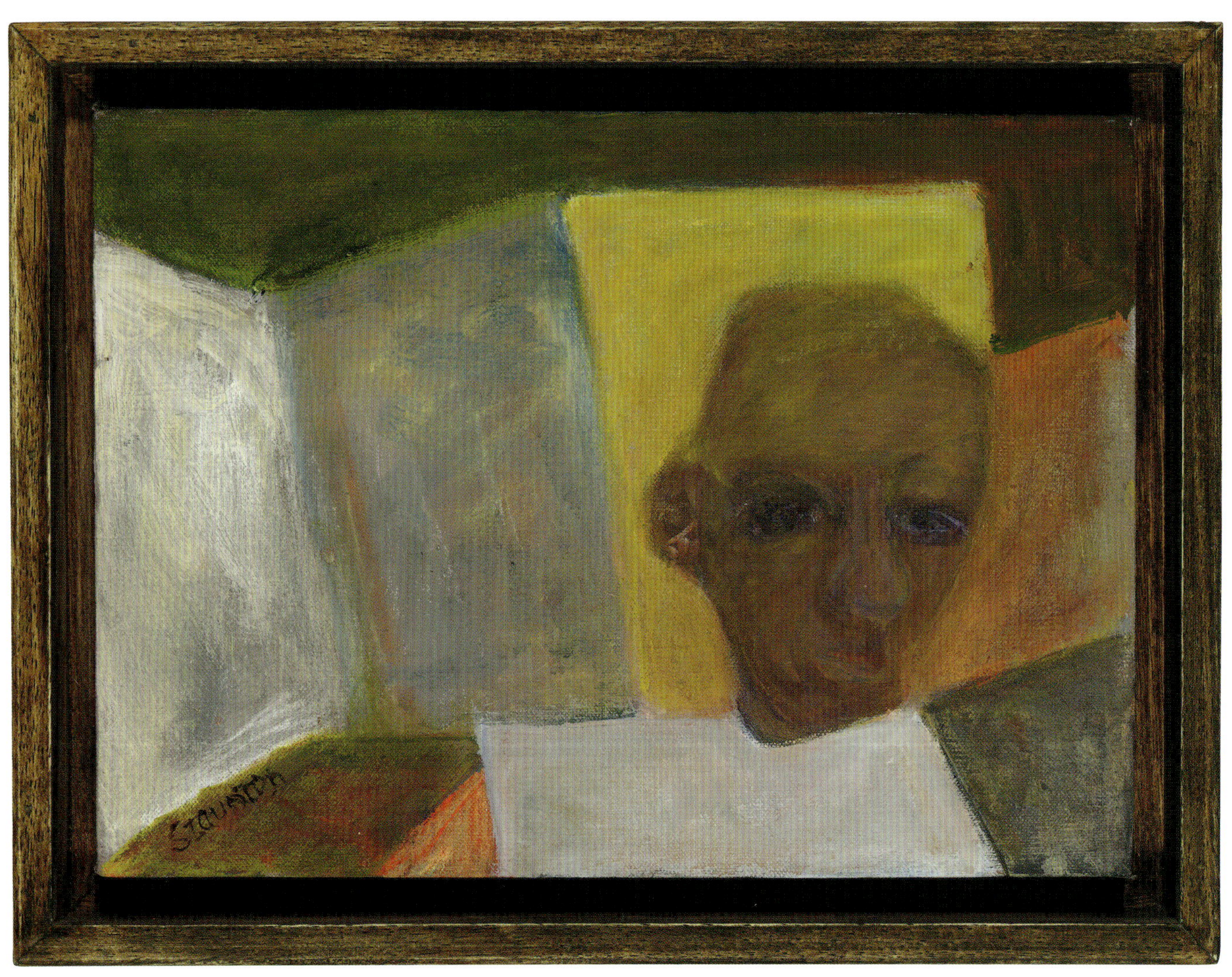

Profile no.2 2012
Synthetic polymer paint on canvas
25.5 x 35.5cm; 31.3 x 41.3 x 5cm (framed)
Collection: The artist

Anxiety 2012
Synthetic polymer paint on canvas board
51 x 40.7cm; 56.2 x 45.8 x 4.3cm (framed)
Purchased 2014 with funds from the Estate of Jessica Ellis through the Queensland Art Gallery | Gallery of Modern Art Foundation
Collection: Queensland Art Gallery

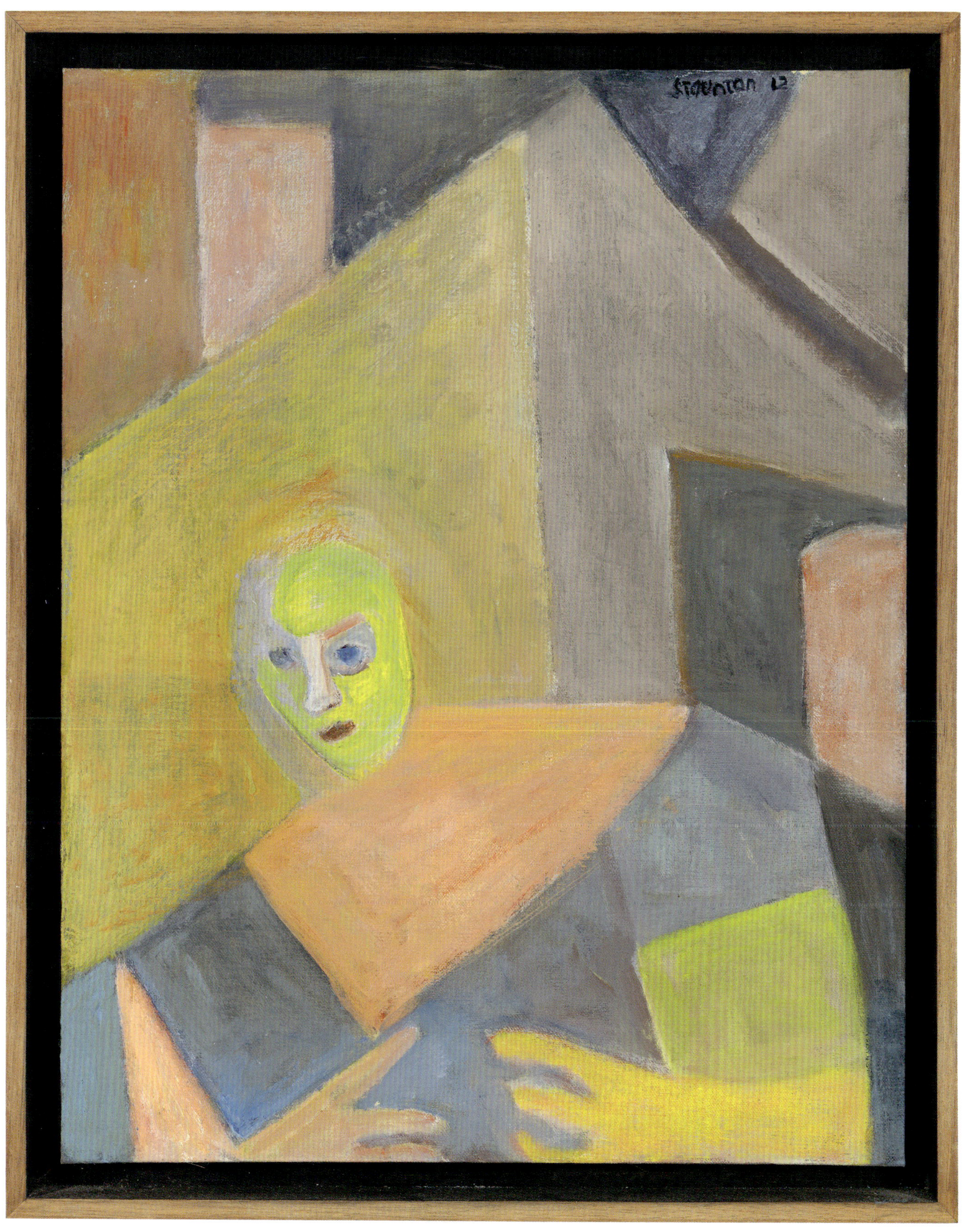
STAUNTON 12

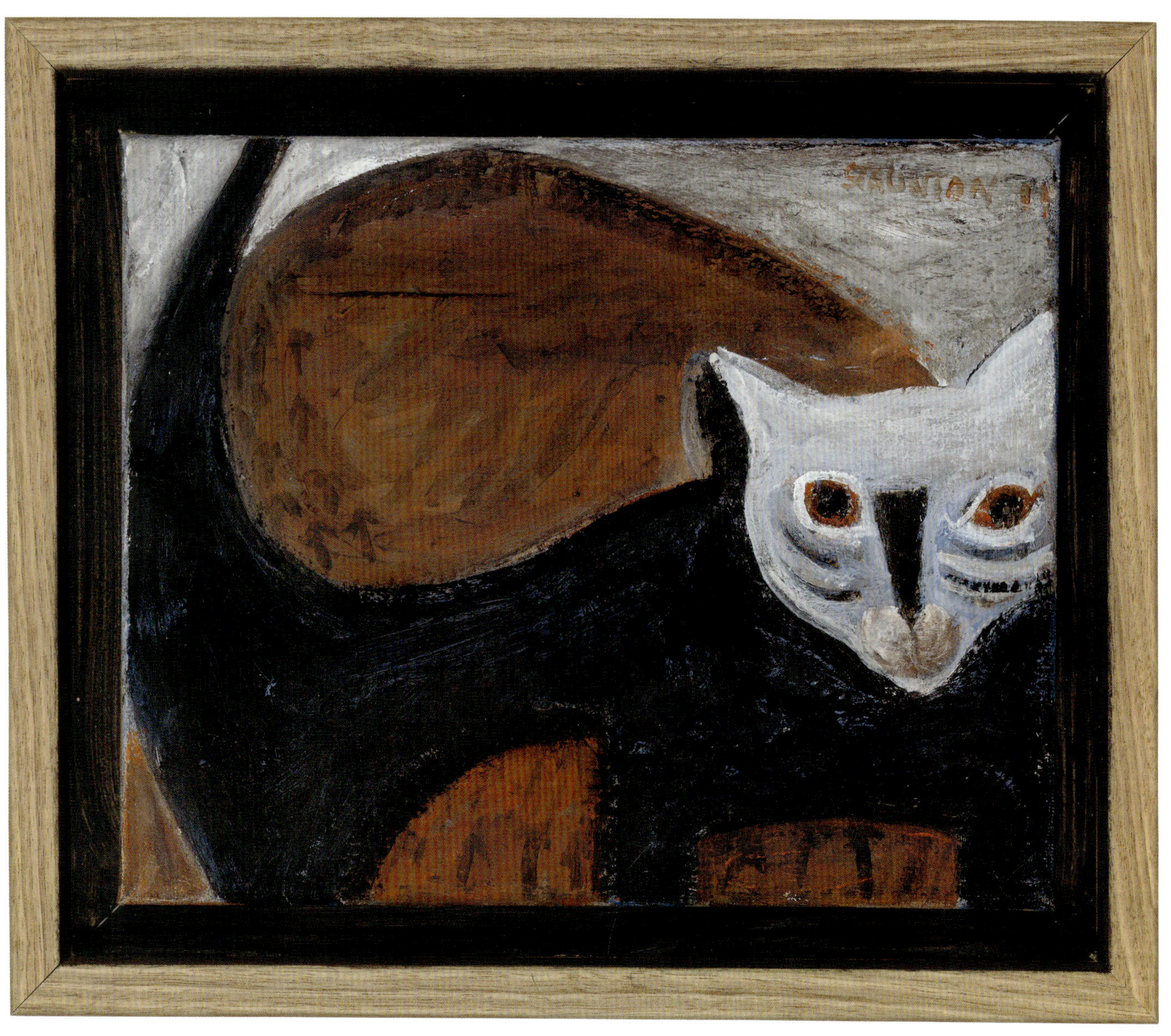

Dowsy cat 2012
Synthetic polymer paint on canvas
20 x 25cm; 26 x 31 x 3.8cm (framed)
Private collection, Brisbane

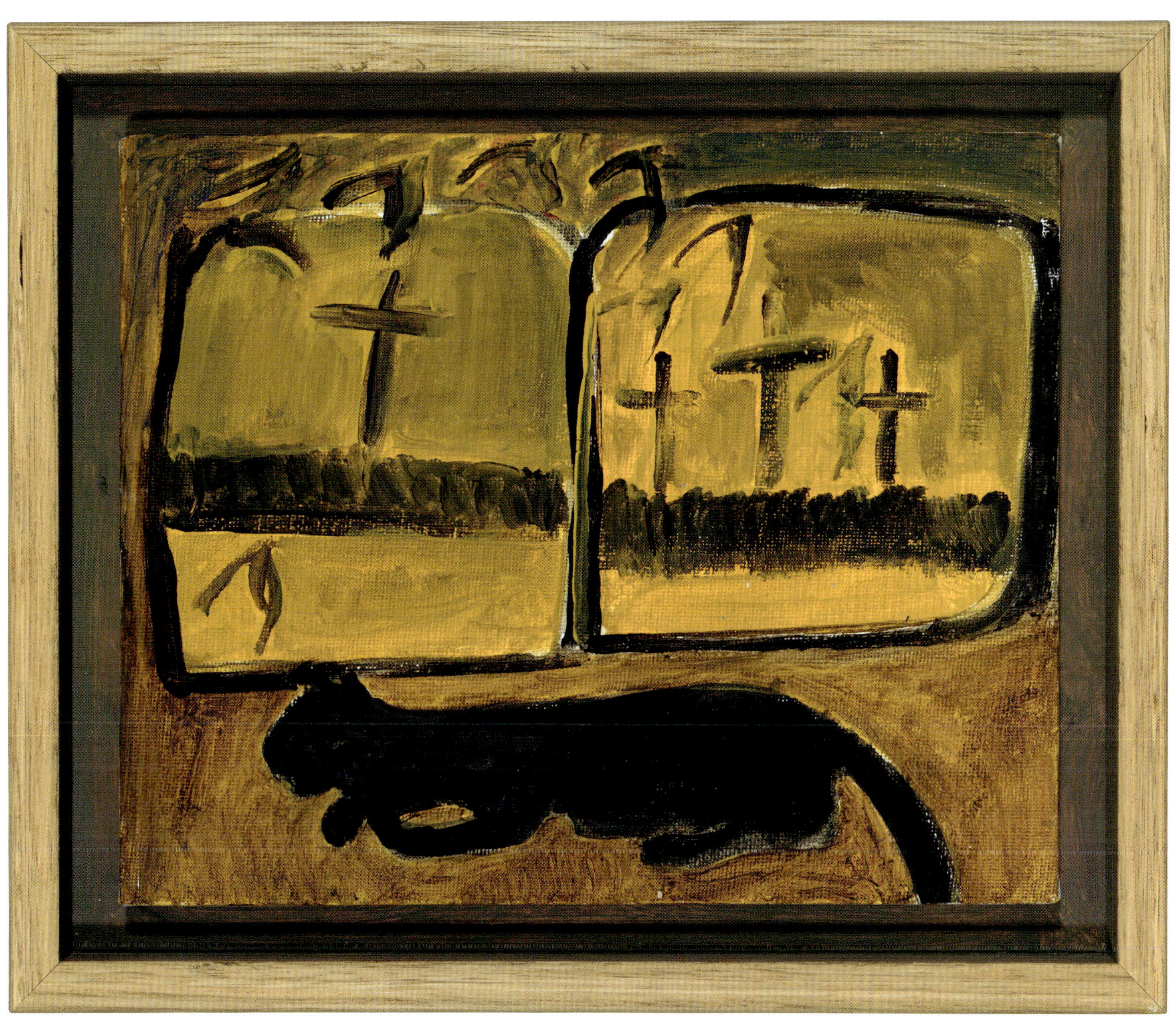

Untitled 2012
Synthetic polymer paint on canvas
20 x 25.5cm; 26 x 31.5 x 3.8cm (framed)
Collection: The artist

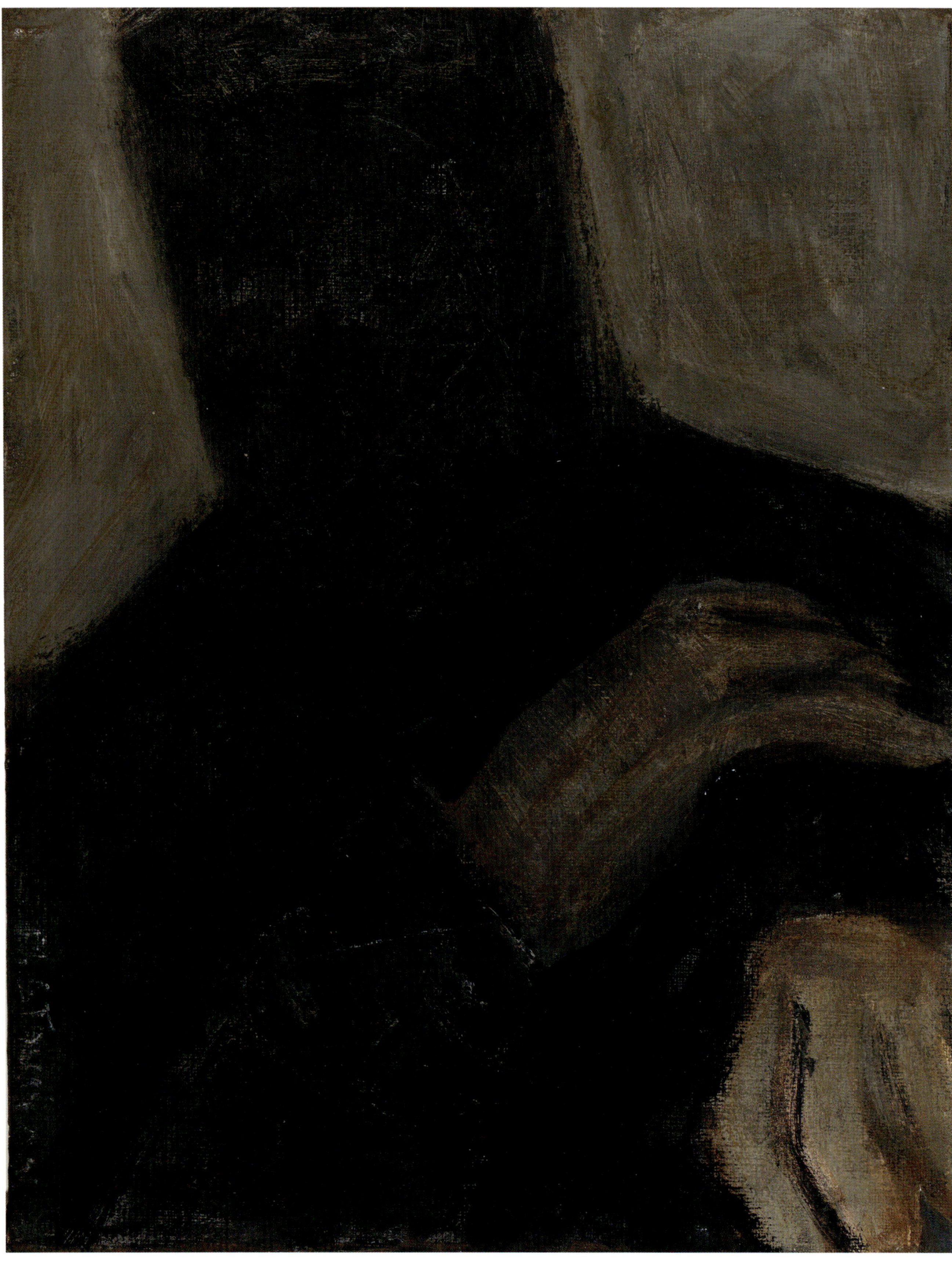

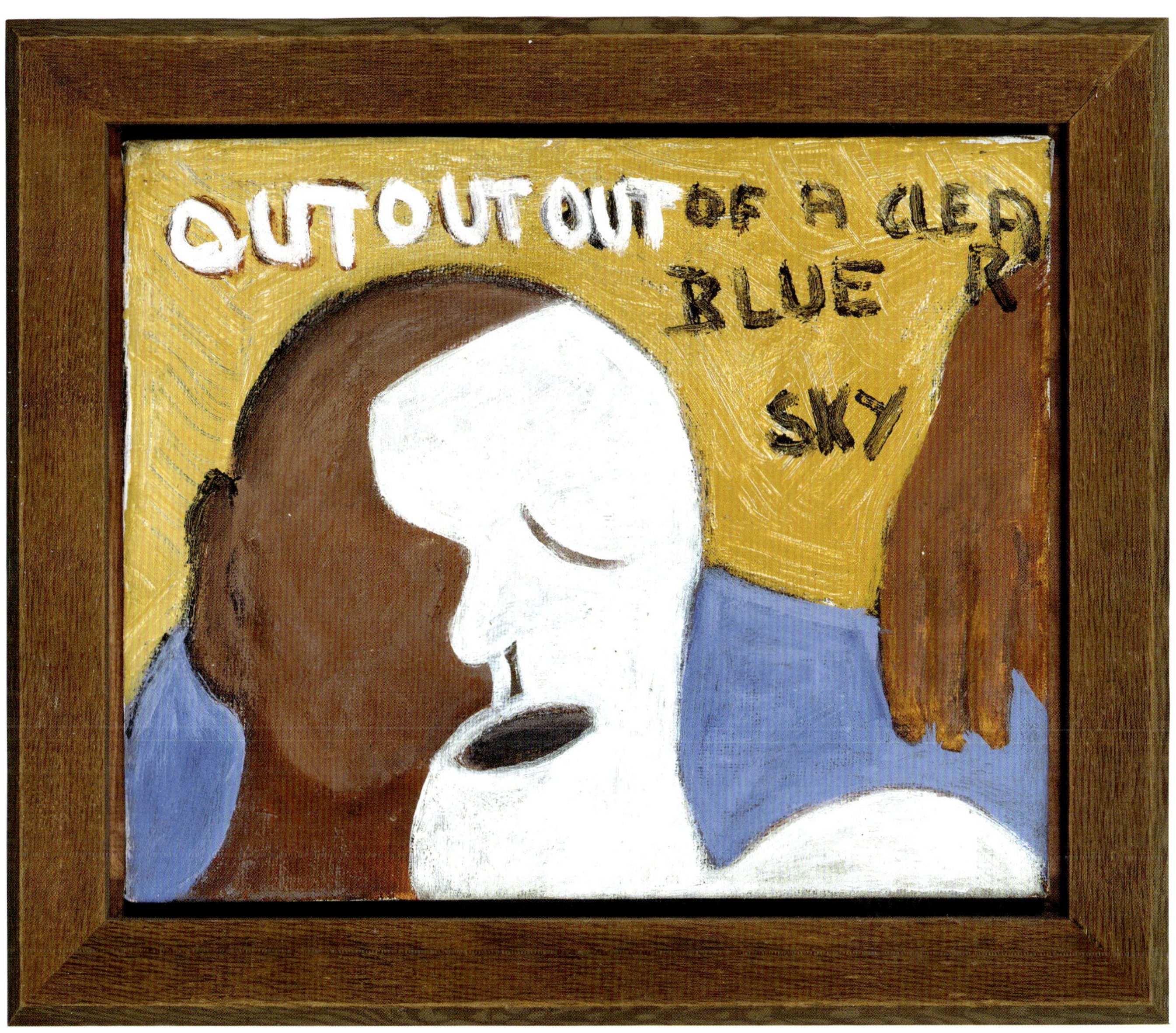

Untitled 2011
Synthetic polymer paint on canvas
25.5 x 20.5cm
Syd Williams Collection

Out of a clear blue sky 2013
Synthetic polymer paint on canvas
20 x 25cm; 27.3 x 32.5 x 4.4cm (framed)
Purchased 2014. Queensland Art Gallery | Gallery of Modern Art
Collection: Queensland Art Gallery

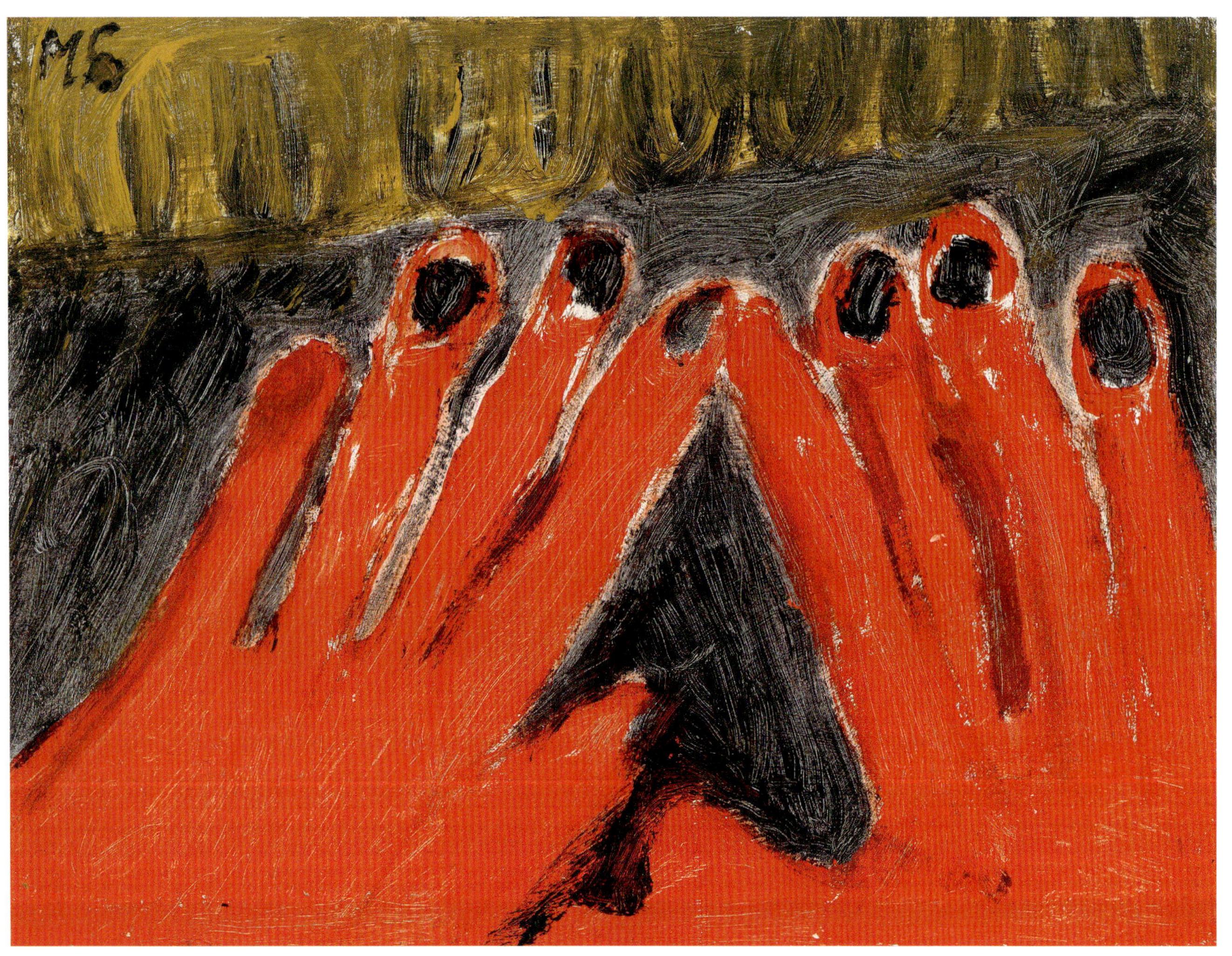

Fingers (detail) 2013
Synthetic polymer paint on wood
15 x 20cm; 25.4 x 30.2 x 3cm (framed)
Collection: The artist

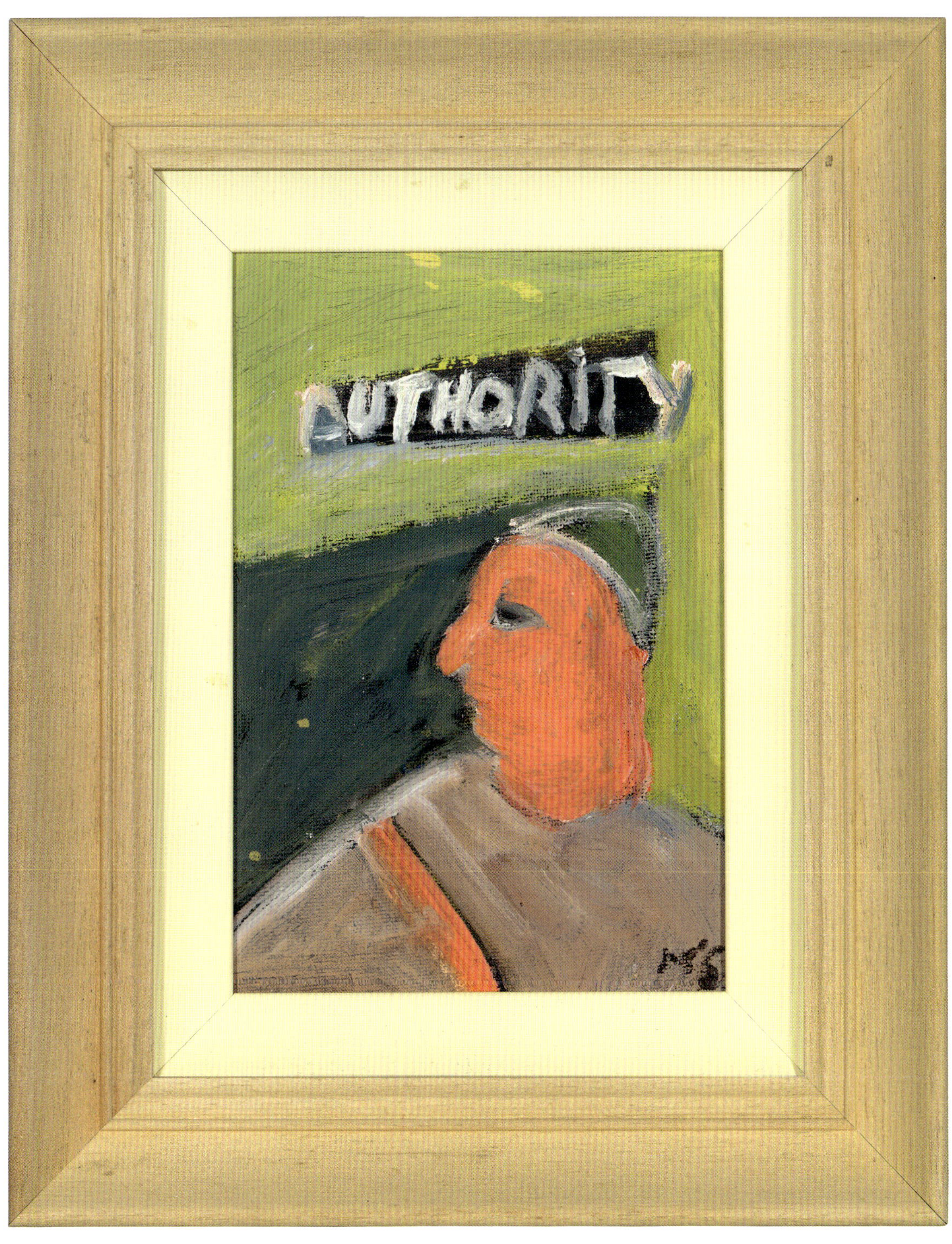

Authority 2013
Synthetic polymer paint on canvas board
17 x 11.7cm; 27.6 x 22.7 x 3.5cm (framed)
Collection: The artist

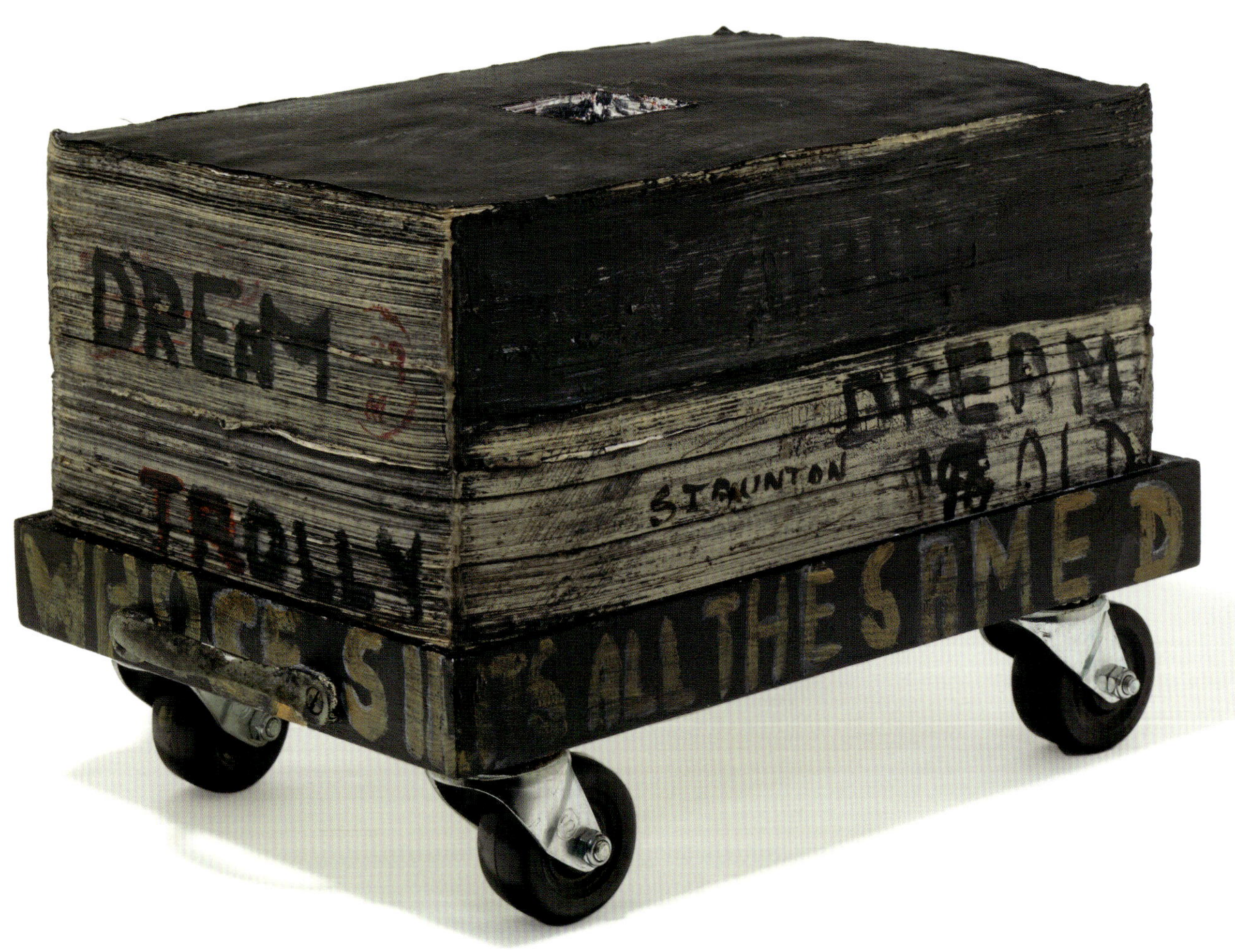

Dream trolly 2013
Paper, glue, wood, metal and plastic with synthetic polymer paint
22 x 37.8 x 23.5cm (irreg.)
Gordon Darling Australia Pacific Print Fund 2014
Collection: National Gallery of Australia, Canberra

Hospital ward (detail) 2013
Synthetic polymer paint on canvas
51 x 40.8cm; 56 x 45.8 x 5cm (framed)
Collection: The artist

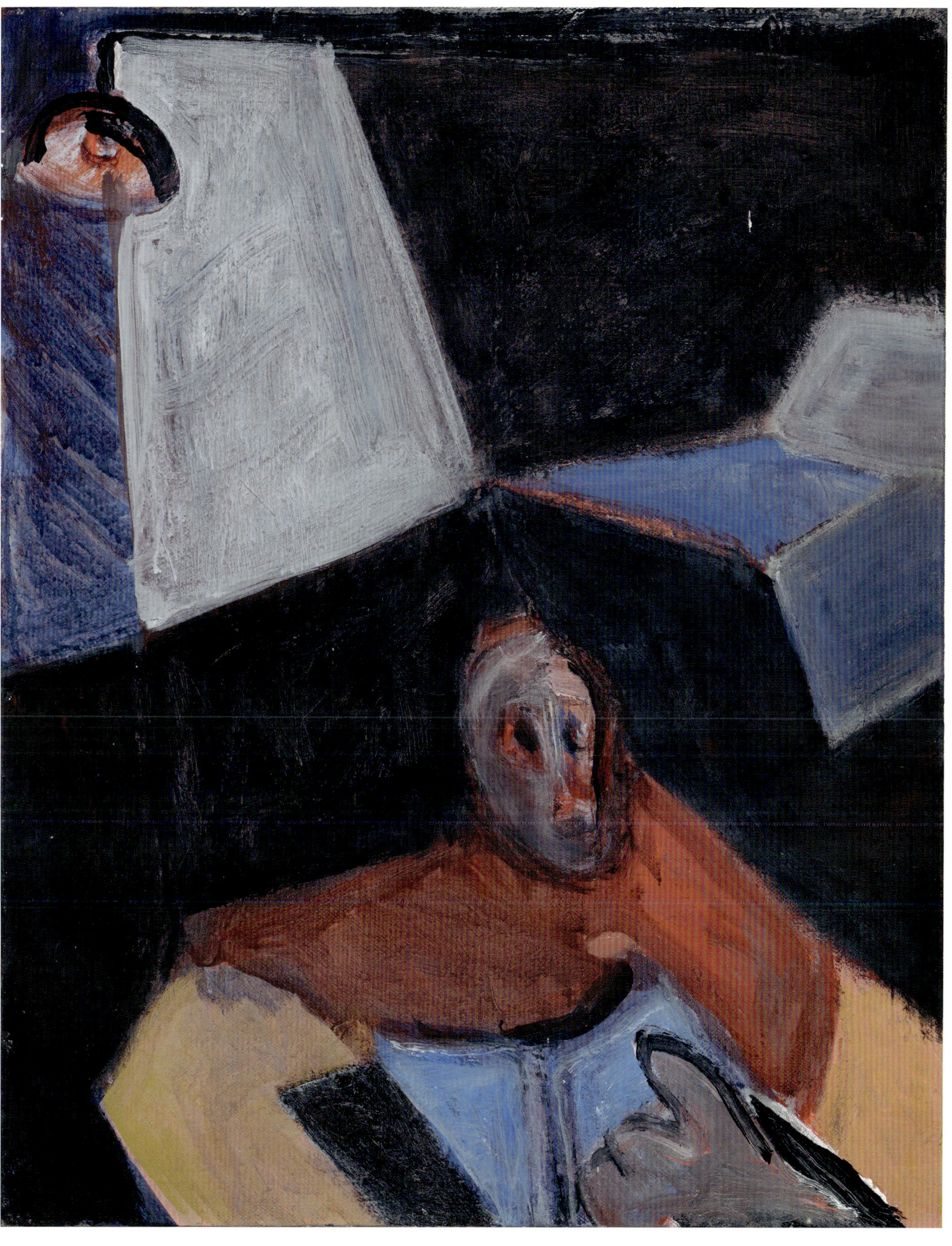

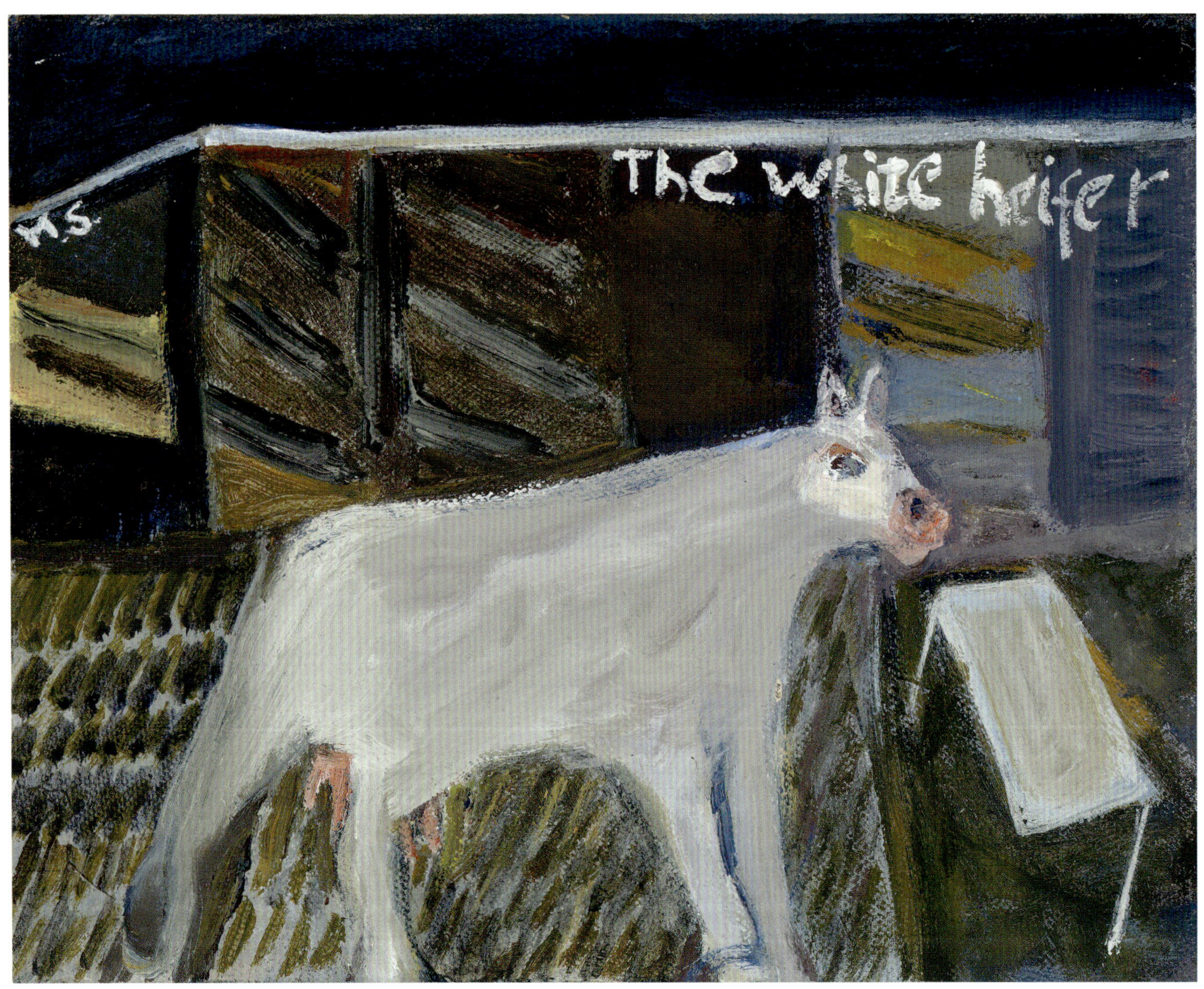

The white heifer (detail) 2014
Synthetic polymer paint on canvas
20.2 x 25.7cm; 25.2 x 30.7 x 3.7cm (framed)
Collection: The artist

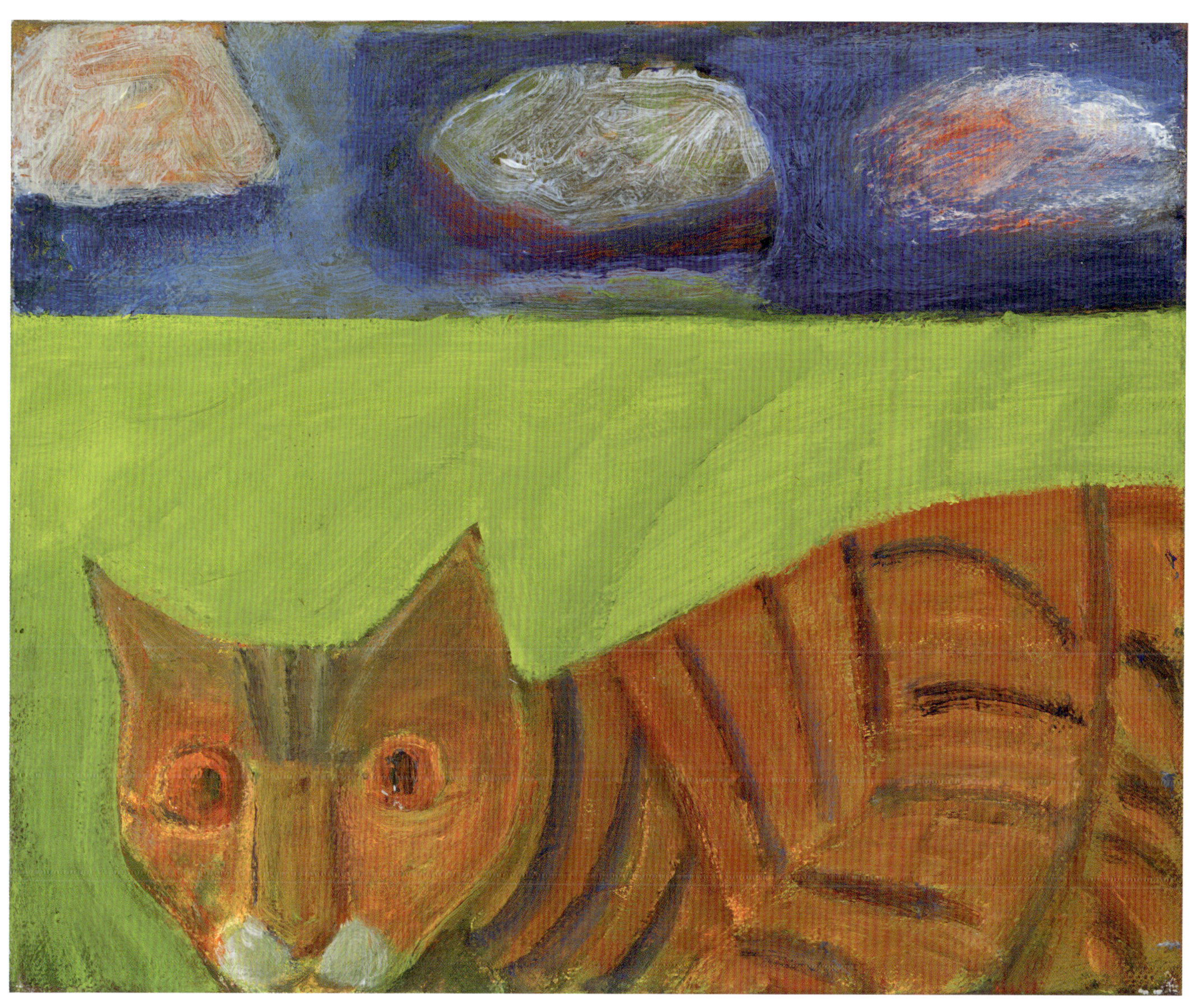

Cat with storm clouds (detail) 2014
Synthetic polymer paint on canvas
20.3 x 25.2cm; 25.3 x 30.2 x
3.7cm (framed)
Collection: The artist

CATALOGUE OF WORKS

Works are listed in chronological order. Dimensions are given in centimetres (cm), height preceding width, followed by depth.

August 1966
Oil and synthetic polymer paint on composition board
122.5 x 184cm; 124.5 x 186cm (framed)
Collection: The artist
p.17

Easter 1967
Oil on composition board
122 x 122cm; 123.4 x 123.6 x 3.5cm (framed)
Gift of the artist, 1992
Queensland University of Technology Art Collection, Brisbane
p.30

Peripheral green, blue 1968
Oil and synthetic polymer paint on composition board
91.5 x 122cm; 94.8 x 125 x 3.5cm (framed)
Private collection, Brisbane
p.31

Untitled 1973
Paper collage on canvas
151 x 173cm
Purchased 1995. Queensland Art Gallery Foundation
Collection: Queensland Art Gallery
p.21

Assemblage with plank 1988
Wood, card, paint and paper
152 x 179 x 13.5cm (irreg.)
Purchased 1992
Collection: Queensland Art Gallery
p.32

Chair with packing case 1993
Painted wood and metal
110 x 74 x 45.5cm (irreg.)
Purchased 2000.
Collection: University of Queensland, Brisbane
p.33

Armature 2 1999
Synthetic polymer paint and wire on plywood
138.3 x 122.4cm (irreg.); 140 x 124.5cm x 5.5cm (framed)
Collection: The artist
p.40

Hide 1 2002
Painted wood, metal, rope and cloth tape
189 x 90 x 88cm (irreg.)
Collection: The artist
p.38

Hide 2 2002
Painted wood, metal, rope and cloth tape
227 x 82 x 78cm (irreg.)
Collection: The artist
p.38

Key 2002
Wood, card, felt, metal, plastic, cloth-bound card and synthetic polymer paint on composition board
84 x 40.8 x 9.2cm (irreg.)
Collection: Michael and Kylie Rayner, Brisbane
p.39

Numbers game 2002
Painted metal, ink bottles and timber box
90 x 90 x 10cm
Purchased 2006 through the Betty Quelhurst Fund
Queensland University of Technology Art Collection, Brisbane
p.37

Romantic doubt 2004
Painted wood, wood, metal, synthetic polymer paint, ink and glue on composition board
3 units: 61 x 61 16.5cm; 61.5 x 61.4 x 11cm; 62 x 66 x 11cm (irreg.)
Private collection
p.34–6

Reprise c.2007
Synthetic polymer paint on composition board
91.6 x 61.2cm; 95 x 64.3 x 6cm (framed)
Collection: The artist
p.46

Immigrant 2008
Synthetic polymer paint on card
23 x 26cm; 25.5 x 28.5 x 2.6cm (framed)
Collection: The artist
p.47

Amputee 2010
Synthetic polymer paint on canvas
25 x 20.5cm; 28.5 x 23.5 x 6cm (framed)
Private collection
p.55

Game 2010
Synthetic polymer paint on canvas
61 x 50.7cm; 64 x 54 x 5cm (framed)
Collection: The artist
p.50

Men's business 2010
Synthetic polymer paint on canvas
60.8 x 50.7cm; 64.1 x 54 x 4.9cm (framed)
Collection: The artist
p.51

No one said 2010
Synthetic polymer paint on canvas
60.5 x 60cm; 64 x 63.4 x 5cm (framed)
Purchased 2014 with funds from the Estate of Jessica Ellis through the Queensland Art Gallery | Gallery of Modern Art Foundation
Collection: Queensland Art Gallery
p.49

They say 2010
Synthetic polymer paint on canvas
29.5 x 24.4cm; 38 x 32.8 x 2.2cm (framed)
Purchased 2014 with funds from the Estate of Jessica Ellis through the Queensland Art Gallery | Gallery of Modern Art Foundation
Collection: Queensland Art Gallery
p.48

Word 2010
Wood, cloth-bound card, tin, wire and synthetic polymer paint
21.5 x 34.4 x 7.8cm
Collection: University of Queensland, Brisbane
Gift of Michael Rayner, AM through the Australian Government's Cultural Gifts Program, 2014.
p.58

Yo 2010
Paper, metal, paint, ink, composition board, paintbrush and canvas board on wood
21 x 36 x 5cm
Private collection, Brisbane
p.59

Apprentice 2011
Synthetic polymer paint on canvas
25 x 20cm
Purchased 2011
Griffith University Art Collection
p.53

Solitary 2011
Gouache on canvas
25 x 20cm
Purchased 2011
Griffith University Art Collection
p.52

Untitled 2011
Synthetic polymer paint on canvas
25.5 x 20.5cm
Syd Williams Collection
p.72

Allegory 2012
Synthetic polymer paint on canvas
25.2 x 20.1cm; 31.4 x 26 x 3.8cm (framed)
Collection: The artist
p.13

Anxiety 2012
Synthetic polymer paint on canvas board
51 x 40.7cm; 56.2 x 45.8 x 4.3cm (framed)
Purchased 2014 with funds from the Estate of Jessica Ellis through the Queensland Art Gallery | Gallery of Modern Art Foundation
Collection: Queensland Art Gallery
p.69

Base camp 2012
Synthetic polymer paint on canvas
20 x 25cm; 26.5 x 31.5 x 3.5cm (framed)
Collection: The artist
p.54

Dowsy cat 2012
Synthetic polymer paint on canvas
20 x 25cm; 26 x 31 x 3.8cm (framed)
Private collection, Brisbane
p.70

Flake 2012
Synthetic polymer paint on canvas
19.5 x 24.3cm; 23.5 x 28.5 x 2.7cm (framed)
Private collection, Brisbane
p.60

Postcard for Emily Dickinson 2012
Synthetic polymer paint on canvas board
16.9 x 11.9cm; 23.2 x 18.2 x 2.5cm (framed)
Private collection, Los Angeles
p.61

Postcard for Graham Greene 2012
Synthetic polymer paint on canvas board
11.8 x 17cm; 18 x 23.2 x 1.4cm (framed)
Private collection
p.62

Postcard for Kafka 2012
Synthetic polymer paint on canvas board
12.5 x 17.6cm; 21.5 x 27.5 x 4.5cm frame
Collection: Dr Morris Low, Brisbane
p.63

Postcard for Samuel Beckett 2012
Synthetic polymer paint on canvas
25 x 20.5cm; 33 x 28 x 5.5cm (framed)
The Paul Eliadis Collection of Contemporary Art, Brisbane
p.64

Postcard for Stevie Smith 2012
Synthetic polymer paint on canvas
20.4 x 25.4cm; 26 x 31.2 x 3.7cm (framed)
Collection: The artist
p.65

Postcard for Tiny Tim 2012
Synthetic polymer paint on canvas
8.2 x 11.8cm; 13 x 16.4 x 2.5cm (framed)
Private collection, Brisbane
p.66

Profile no.1 2012
Synthetic polymer paint on canvas
30.5 x 25cm; 36 x 30.8 x 5cm (framed)
Collection: Gino Milani, Brisbane
p.67

Profile no.2 2012
Synthetic polymer paint on canvas
25.5 x 35.5cm; 31.3 x 41.3 x 5cm (framed)
Collection: The artist
p.68

The eye of the storm 2012
Synthetic polymer paint on canvas
40.8 x 50.8cm; 43 x 53.2 x 4.5cm (framed)
Collection: The artist
p.56

The reader 2012
Synthetic polymer paint on canvas
76 x 61.2cm; 81 x 66.5 x 4.5cm (framed)
Syd Williams Collection
p.57

Untitled 2012
Synthetic polymer paint on canvas
20 x 25.5cm; 26 x 31.5 x 3.8cm (framed)
Collection: The artist
p.71

Authority 2013
Synthetic polymer paint on canvas board
17 x 11.7cm; 27.6 x 22.7 x 3.5cm (framed)
Collection: The artist
p.75

Dream trolly 2013
Paper, glue, wood, metal and plastic with synthetic polymer paint
22 x 37.8 x 23.5cm (irreg.)
Gordon Darling Australia Pacific Print Fund 2014
Collection: National Gallery of Australia, Canberra
p.76

Fingers 2013
Synthetic polymer paint on wood
15 x 20cm; 25.4 x 30.2 x 3cm (framed)
Collection: The artist
p.74

Hospital ward 2013
Synthetic polymer paint on canvas
51 x 40.8cm; 56 x 45.8 x 5cm (framed)
Collection: The artist
p.77

Out of a clear blue sky 2013
Synthetic polymer paint on canvas
20 x 25cm; 27.3 x 32.5 x 4.4cm (framed)
Purchased 2014. Queensland Art Gallery | Gallery of Modern Art
Collection: Queensland Art Gallery
p.9, 73

Sunflowers 2013
Synthetic polymer paint on canvas
51 x 40.5cm; 56 x 45.5 x 5cm (framed)
Purchased 2014 with funds from the Estate of the late Kathleen Elizabeth Mowle through the Queensland Art Gallery | Gallery of Modern Art Foundation
Collection: Queensland Art Gallery
p.28

Cat with storm clouds 2014
Synthetic polymer paint on canvas
20.3 x 25.2cm; 25.3 x 30.2 x 3.7cm (framed)
Collection: The artist
p.79

The white heifer 2014
Synthetic polymer paint on canvas
20.2 x 25.7cm; 25.2 x 30.7 x 3.7cm (framed)
Collection: The artist
p.78

Works on paper

All works are in the artist's collection unless otherwise stated.

Self portrait c.1960
Graphite
38.5 x 25cm

Untitled 1976
Paper collage
27.2 x 23.6cm
The James C Sourris, AM, Collection, Brisbane
p.19

Untitled 1976
Paper collage
27.4 x 24.1cm
The James C Sourris, AM, Collection, Brisbane
p.19

Untitled 1976
Paper collage
27.8 x 24.2cm
The James C Sourris, AM, Collection, Brisbane
p.19

Self portrait c.1980
Ink
31 x 23cm
p.14

Self portrait c.1980
Ink
31 x 23cm
p.14

Self portrait c.1980
Ink
31 x 23cm
p.14

Woman in motion c.1995
Synthetic polymer paint
112.2 x 75cm
p.6

Untiled (square) 1995
Etching, ed. 5/10
14 x 10.5cm
p.22

Untitled (triangle) 1995
Etching, ed. 5/10
14 x 10.5cm
p.22

Evasive bird c.1999
Monotype
10.5 x 16cm

Monotype (Dancing bird) c.1999
Monotype
29.5 x 40cm

Monotype (Landscape with safety pin) c.1999
Monotype
16 x 22cm
p.25

Monotype (Mother bird) c.1999
Monotype
15.5 x 22cm
p.24

Monotype (Splashing birds) c.1999
Monotype
28 x 38cm

Nodding bird c.1999
Relief print
14 x 25.5cm
p.23

N.Y. 11 Sept 01 2001
Monotype
16 x 24.5cm
p.42

N.Y. 11 Sept 01 2001
Monotype
16 x 24.5cm
p.42

N.Y. 11 Sept 01 2001
Monotype
16 x 24.5cm
p.43

N.Y. 11 Sept 01 2001
Monotype
16 x 24.5cm
p.43

Untitled suite (Closet) c.2001
Etching, collage
3 sheets: 17 x 13cm (each)
p.10

Descending safety pin 2002
Monotype
10.5 x 10.5cm

Reclining safety pin 2002
Monotype
10.5 x 10.5cm

Safety pins and body parts c.2002
Etching
17 x 14cm
p.44

Untitled (Safety pin) c.2002
Monotype
21.5 x 33cm

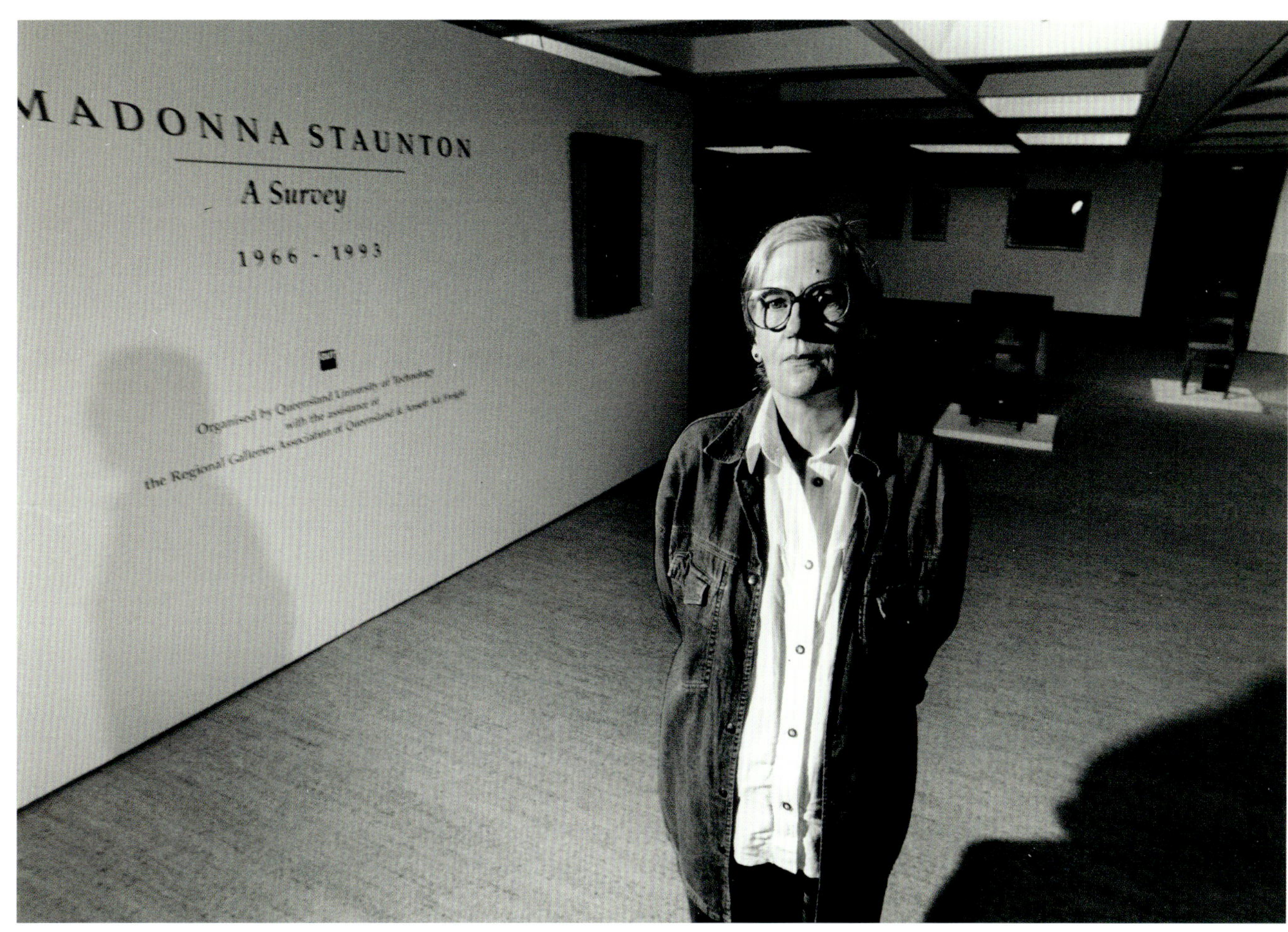

The artist at her exhibition 'Madonna Staunton: A Survey 1966–1993', Queensland Art Gallery, organised by Queensland University of Technology, 1994
Collection: Queensland Art Gallery | Gallery of Modern Art Research Library

Floating lovers no.2 c.2005
Monotype
10 x 13cm
p.41

Mask with still life c.2005
Monotype
29 x 28cm
p.45

Kitchen blues 2009
Gouache
9.8 x 14.8cm
Collection: Michael and Kylie Rayner, Brisbane
cover, p.27

Distressed text n.d.
Photocopy
26 x 18cm

Distressed text n.d.
Photo-etching
30 x 21cm

Additional material

Madge Staunton
Australia QLD 1917–86
(Colour theory exercise book) c. 1948
Graphite, ink, collage, gouache, on cloth-hinged and stapled interleaved book with printed cover
24 pages: 24.6 x 31.3cm (closed, landscape)

EXHIBITION HISTORY

MADONNA STAUNTON

1938 Born Murwillumbah, New South Wales. Lives in Brisbane, Queensland

Selected individual exhibitions

2013 'Dream Trolly', Grahame Galleries + Editions, Brisbane

2012 'New Works', Milani Gallery, Brisbane

2010 'Homework', Milani Gallery, Brisbane

2006 'Breaking the Line', Bellas Milani Gallery, Brisbane

2004 'Difficult Accord', Bellas Milani Gallery, Brisbane

2003 'Madonna Staunton', Institute of Modern Art, Brisbane

'A Personal Survey', Bellas Gallery, Brisbane

2000 'Monotypes', Bellas Gallery, Brisbane

'Homage to Erik Satie', De Montfort University, Leicester, United Kingdom

1999 'Madonna Staunton', Metro Arts, Brisbane

1998 'New Works – Armatures', Bellas Gallery, Brisbane

1997 'Winged Archive', Bellas Gallery, Brisbane

1996 'Patience and the Provoked', Sutton Gallery, Melbourne

1995 '1–6 Recent Works', Bellas Gallery, Brisbane

1994 'Madonna Staunton: A Survey 1966–1993', Queensland Art Gallery, Brisbane; Perc Tucker Regional Gallery, Townsville

'Madonna Staunton', Bellas Gallery, Brisbane

1993 'Paradigms', Sutton Gallery, Melbourne

1992 'Iconic Images', Bellas Gallery, Brisbane

1991 'Recent Works', Gary Anderson Gallery, Sydney

1989 'Recent Works: Assemblage – Collage', Bellas Gallery, Brisbane

1988 'Madonna Staunton: Collages', Gary Anderson Gallery, Sydney

1984 'Madonna Staunton: Collages', Gary Anderson Gallery, Sydney

1983 'Madonna Staunton', Ray Hughes Gallery, Brisbane

1980 'Madonna Staunton: Collage Repeat Collage', Ray Hughes Gallery, Brisbane

'Madonna Staunton: Assemblage, Drawing Collage', Ray Hughes Gallery, Brisbane

1979 'Madonna Staunton: A Recent Work', Institute of Modern Art, Brisbane

1978 'Madonna Staunton: Collage', Ray Hughes Gallery, Brisbane

1977 'Madonna Staunton: 50 Collages', Ray Hughes Gallery, Brisbane

1976 'Madonna Staunton', Ray Hughes Gallery, Brisbane

Selected group exhibitions

2013 'NEW 2013: Selected Recent Acquisitions', University of Queensland Art Museum, Brisbane

'Born to Concrete: Visual Poetry from the Collections of Heide Museum of Modern Art and The University of Queensland', University of Queensland Art Museum, Brisbane

2012 'Bookplates Unbound', The Studio, West End, Brisbane

'Lessons in History Vol 11 – Democracy', Grahame Galleries + Editions, Brisbane

2011 'Black Elastic, Two Umbrellas, a Mint Leaf and Wheels', Monash University Museum of Art, Melbourne

'Born to Concrete: The Heide Collection', Heide Museum of Modern Art, Heide

2010 'A Generosity of Spirit: Recent Australian Women's Art from the QUT Art Collection', Queensland University of Technology Art Museum, Brisbane; Samstag Museum, University of South Australia, Adelaide

'The Navigators', Karen Woodbury Gallery, Melbourne

'2010 National Works on Paper', Mornington Peninsula Regional Gallery, Mornington

'NEW 2010: Selected Recent Acquisitions', University of Queensland Art Museum, Brisbane

'Stick it!!: Collage in Australian Art', National Gallery of Victoria, Melbourne

2009 'Cubism & Australian Art', Heide Museum of Modern Art

2008 'Under the Influence: Art and Music', Queensland University of Technology Art Museum, Brisbane

'The Contemporary Collage: Australian Collage and Assemblage', John Buckley Gallery, Melbourne

'Repeat that again!', University of Queensland Art Museum, Brisbane

2007 'Lessons in History Vol 1', Grahame Galleries + Editions, Brisbane

'The Betty Quelhurst Gift', Queensland University of Technology Art Museum, Brisbane

'The National Gallery of Australia Celebrates 25 Years', National Gallery of Australia, Canberra

'Materiality', Monash University Museum of Art, Clayton

'Transformers: More than Meets the Eye', Queensland University of Technology Art Museum, Brisbane

2006 'La Femme Domestique', Queensland University of Technology Art Museum, Brisbane

'WARNING: Smoking Has Been Linked to Some of the Most Powerful Images of the Twentieth Century', Mornington Peninsula Regional Gallery

2005 'Interesting Times: Focus on Contemporary Australian Art', Museum of Contemporary Art, Sydney

2004 'From the Ephemeral to the Eternal: The Recent Work of Eugene Carchesio, Helen Fuller and Madonna Staunton', University of South Australia Art Museum, Adelaide

'Kurt Schwitters Acquisition and Related Works from the Collection', Art Gallery of New South Wales, Sydney

2003 'Fragments', Queensland Art Gallery, Brisbane

2002 'LxWxH', Brisbane City Gallery, Brisbane

1998 'Fluxus – The International and the Avant Garde', Queensland Art Gallery

'Artists' Books', Brisbane City Gallery

'Ex.Cat : An Exhibition About Catholicism', Smith & Stoneley Gallery, Brisbane

1996 'Words', Queensland Art Gallery, Brisbane

'Australia: Familiar and Strange', Seoul Arts Center, Korea

1997 'Now', Bellas Gallery, Brisbane

'New Works on Paper (with Jon Cattapan and Leonard Brown)', Bellas Gallery, Brisbane

'Gramercy International Art Fair', New York

1996 'Reference Points IV', Queensland Art Gallery, Brisbane

1995 'B.I.A. Annual Exhibition', Brisbane Institute of Art, Old Museum Building, Brisbane

'The Paper Makers', Queensland Museum, Brisbane

1994 'group♀', Sutton Gallery, Melbourne

'Carved and Transformed: Artists' Furniture from the Collection', Queensland Art Gallery, Brisbane

1993 'Fluxus and After . . . ', Queensland Art Gallery, Brisbane

1992 'Domino 1', Ian Potter Museum of Art, University of Melbourne

'Abstract: The Non Objective', Museum of Contemporary Art, Brisbane

'Collecting Art: Critic's Choice', Macquarie Galleries, Sydney

'Christmas Show', Sutton Gallery, Melbourne

1991 'The Book and Print Show', The Long Gallery, University of Wollongong; Goulburn Regional Art Gallery; Penrith Regional Gallery and The Lewers Bequest, Emu Plains

'Signals', Bellas Gallery, Brisbane

'From the Landscape: A Review of the Influence of the Landscape in Contemporary Art', Museum of Contemporary Art, Brisbane

'The Artist's Book Show', State Library of Queensland, Brisbane; Mackay City Library; Innisfail Library; Toowoomba Art Gallery

'Contemporary Art Society (Queensland Branch) 1961–73', Brisbane City Hall Art Gallery and Museum, Brisbane

1990 'Mass Media: Mixed Media', Painters' Gallery, Sydney

'Osmosis', Gary Anderson Gallery, Sydney

'Madonna Staunton and Eugene Carchesio: The Theoretical Axis of Happiness', Bellas Gallery, Brisbane

1989 'Assembled Art', The Centre Gallery, Gold Coast; toured 1990 to Tweed River Regional Art Gallery, Murwillumbah

'Group Exhibition', Bellas Gallery, Brisbane

1988 'Charles Page, Madonna Staunton, Normana Wight', Grahame Galleries, Brisbane

'National Women's Art Award', The Centre Gallery, Gold Coast

'A Complementary Caste: A Homage to Women Artists in Queensland, Past and Present', The Centre Gallery, Gold Coast

1987 'Cool, Quiet Art: Recent Works by Leonard Brown, Helen Lillecrapp-Fuller, Madonna Staunton, June Tupicoff', Ipswich City Council Art Gallery

'Winter Exhibition', Gary Anderson Gallery, Sydney

'Painters and Sculptors: Diversity in Contemporary Australian Art', Queensland Art Gallery, Brisbane; Museum of Modern Art, Saitama, Japan

'The Age of Collage', Holdsworth Contemporary Galleries, Sydney

1986 'Works on Paper: 1950 to the Present', 312 Lennox Street Gallery, Melbourne

'Aberdare Prize for Still Life', Ipswich City Council Art Gallery

1985 'The First Exhibition', Ray Hughes Gallery, Sydney

'Queensland Works 1950–1985', University of Queensland Art Museum, Brisbane

'Six New Directions', Queensland Art Gallery, Brisbane

'Sorry – I'm Thinking Aloud', Ray Hughes Gallery, Sydney

'Australian Perspecta 85', Art Gallery of New South Wales, Sydney

1984 'Recent Acquisitions 1981–1983', Brisbane College of Advanced Education, Brisbane

1983 'Australian Perspecta 83', Art Gallery of New South Wales, Sydney

'Acquisitions 1973–1983', University of Queensland Art Museum, Brisbane

'The Collage Show by 10 Artists', Institute of Modern Art, Brisbane

1982 'The Collage Show', Visual Arts Board Regional Development Program No.10, Sydney (touring exhibition): Perc Tucker Regional Gallery, Townsville; Mt Isa Memorial Civic Centre; Mackay City Library; Rockhampton City Art Gallery; Noosa Shire Gallery, Tewantin; Institute of Modern Art, Brisbane; Lismore Regional Gallery; Newcastle Regional Art Gallery; Ivan Dougherty Gallery, Sydney; Wagga Wagga City Art Gallery; Canberra School of Art Gallery; Shepparton Art Gallery; Geelong Art Gallery; Devonport Gallery and Arts Centre; Burnie Regional Art Gallery.

'Georges Invitation Art Award', Georges Gallery, Melbourne

'Airshow', Contemporary Art Society, Adelaide; Dalby Regional Art Gallery, Dalby

1981 'Ray Hughes at Pinacotheca', Pinacotheca Gallery, Melbourne

'Nine Queensland Artists', Perc Tucker Regional Gallery, Townsville

1980 'Drawn and Quartered: Australian Contemporary Paperworks', Art Gallery of South Australia, Adelaide

'Brisbane Women Artists', Kelvin Grove College of Advanced Education, Brisbane

'The Queensland Connection: Ray Hughes Gallery at the Contemporary Art Society', Contemporary Art Society, Adelaide

1979 'MacPherson, Shepherdson, Staunton', University of Queensland Art Museum, Brisbane; [on tour 1979–80] Newcastle Art Gallery; Shepparton Art Gallery; Queen Victoria Museum and Art Gallery, Launceston; Devonport Gallery and Arts Centre; Ararat Art Gallery; Victorian College of the Arts, Melbourne; Fremantle Arts Centre; Museum and Art Galleries of the Northern Territory, Darwin.

'European Dialogue: The Third Biennale of Sydney', Art Gallery of New South Wales, Sydney

1977 'Collage', Ray Hughes Gallery, Brisbane

1976 'Brisbane Paintings Today', Institute of Modern Art, Brisbane

1971 'Contemporary Art Society State Exhibition', Schonell Theatre, Brisbane

1970 'Contemporary Art Society Autumn Exhibition', David Jones Valley Auditorium, Brisbane

1969 'Contemporary Art Society Annual Interstate Warana Exhibition', SGIO Theatre Foyer, Brisbane

1968 'Contemporary Art Society Winter Exhibition', TC Beirne's Auditorium, Brisbane

1967 'Contemporary Art Society Annual Interstate Exhibition', David Jones Valley Auditorium, Brisbane

1966 'Contemporary Art Society Winter Exhibition', Finney's Auditorium, Brisbane

'HC Richards Memorial Prize', Queensland Art Gallery, Brisbane

1965 'LJ Harvey Memorial Prize', Queensland Art Gallery, Brisbane

1964 'Contemporary Art Society Annual Local Exhibition', Finney's Auditorium, Brisbane

1961 'Royal Queensland Art Society 73rd Annual Exhibition', Eagers Retail Showroom, Brisbane

1960 'Royal Queensland Art Society 72nd Annual Exhibition', The Australian Hotel, Brisbane

1959 'Royal Queensland Art Society 71st Annual Exhibition', The Australian Hotel, Brisbane

1966–1971 Contemporary Art Society', Brisbane

1956–1961 'Royal Queensland Art Society Annual Exhibition', Brisbane

Public collections

Allen, Allen and Hemsley Collection

Artbank, Sydney

Art Gallery of New South Wales, Sydney

Art Gallery of Western Australia, Perth

Bendigo Art Gallery

Benalla Art Gallery

Brisbane City Gallery

Burnie Regional Art Gallery

Griffith University, Brisbane

Monash University, Melbourne

National Gallery of Australia, Canberra

National Gallery of Victoria, Melbourne

Parliament House, Canberra

Perc Tucker Regional Gallery, Townsville

Queensland Art Gallery | Gallery of Modern Art, Brisbane

Queensland University of Technology, Brisbane

University of Queensland, Brisbane

Awards

1996 Medal of the Order of Australia

1990 Visual Arts/Craft Board, Development Grant

1988–1989 Selected National Women's Art Award, Centre Gallery, Gold Coast

1986 Visual Arts Board Overseas Studio Residency, Tokyo (not undertaken)

ACKNOWLEDGMENTS

Sponsored by

Glencore

Lenders

The Queensland Art Gallery I Gallery of Modern Art wishes to thank Madonna Staunton for generously making available works from her own collection, as well as the following lenders who provided works for inclusion in the exhibition:

Institutional lenders

Griffith University Art Collection, Brisbane
National Gallery of Australia, Canberra
Queensland University of Technology Art Collection, Brisbane
University of Queensland Art Museum, Brisbane

Private lenders

The Paul Eliadis Collection of Contemporary Art, Brisbane
Dr Morris Low, Brisbane
Gino Milani, Brisbane
Michael and Kylie Rayner, Brisbane
The James C Sourris, AM, Collection, Brisbane
Syd Williams Collection

And other private lenders who wish to remain anonymous

Project support

The Gallery thanks the following individuals for their assistance with the project:
Josh Milani, Zoe De Luca, and Tim Walsh, Milani Gallery, Brisbane
Noreen Grahame, Grahame Galleries + Editions, Brisbane

The Gallery also acknowledges the following institutions for their assistance:
Naomi Evans and Michael Barnett, Griffith University Art Gallery and Griffith University Art Collection
Roger Butler, Pam Bailey and Elspeth Pitt, National Gallery of Australia, Canberra
Vanessa Van Ooyen, Megan Williams, and Sheryn Smith, QUT Art Museum and William Robinson Gallery
Dr Campbell Gray, Michele Helmrich, Kath Kerswell, and Matt Malone, University of Queensland Art Museum

Executive Management Team

Chris Saines, CNZM, Director
Celestine Doyle, Deputy Director, Marketing, Development and Commercial Services
Maud Page, Deputy Director, Collection and Exhibitions
Simon Wright, Assistant Director, Learning and Public Engagement

Curator

Peter McKay, Curator, Contemporary Australian Art

Curatorial Support

Julie Ewington, Curatorial Manager, Australian Art (until April 2014)

Project team

Helen Bovey, A/Head, Access, Education and Regional Services
and staff

Izabella Chabrowska, Retail Manager, QAGOMA Stores
and staff

Tamsin Cull, A/Head of Public Programs, Children's Art Centre and Membership (until May 2014)
Jennie Lane, QAGOMA Members Coordinator
Fiona Neill, Public Programs Coordinator
and staff

Tarragh Cunningham, Exhibition Manager
Teresa Nielsen, Project Assistant

Andrew Dudley, Head of Registration
Susie Quinn, Registrar, Collections
and staff

Judy Gunning, Information and Publishing Services Manager
and staff

Dominique Jones, A/Foundation Manager
and staff

Bronwyn Klepp, Principal Marketing and Advertising Officer
Zoe Graham, Principal Sponsorship and Business Development Officer
Amelia Gundelach, Senior Media Officer
Dan Cameron, Senior Communication Officer
and staff

Michael O'Sullivan, Design Manager
Katrina Bell, Senior Exhibition Designer
Grace Liu, Exhibition Designer

Amanda Pagliarino, Head of Conservation
Anne Carter, Conservator, Paintings
Gillian Osmond, Conservator, Paintings
Samantha Shellard, Conservator, Works on Paper
Robert Zilli, Conservation Framer
Nicholas Cosgrove, Conservation Assistant
Elizabeth Thompson, Conservator

Publication

Editing: Christina Pagliaro, Senior Editor
Additional editing: Stephanie Kennard, Assistant Editor
Design: Sally Nall, Graphic Designer
Artwork photography: Natasha Harth, Photographer
Ephemera photography: Mark Sherwood, Assistant Photographer

Publisher

Queensland Art Gallery | Gallery of Modern Art
Stanley Place, South Bank, Brisbane
PO Box 3686, South Brisbane
Queensland 4101 Australia
qagoma.qld.gov.au

Published for 'Madonna Staunton: Out of a Clear Blue Sky', an exhibition organised by the Queensland Art Gallery | Gallery of Modern Art (QAGOMA) and held at QAG, Brisbane, Australia, 30 August 2014 – 1 March 2015.

Curator: Peter McKay, Curator, Contemporary Australian Art

National Library of Australia Cataloguing-in-Publication entry

Authors: McKay, Peter, curator;
Staunton, Madonna, artist.
Title: Madonna Staunton: out of a clear blue sky / Queensland Art Gallery / Gallery of Modern Art.
ISBN: 9781921503658 (paperback)
Subjects: Staunton, Madonna–Exhibitions.
Art, Australian–21st century–Exhibitions.
Other Authors/Contributors:
Queensland Art Gallery, author.
Gallery of Modern Art, author.
Dewey Number: 709.94

Notes on the publication

Dimensions of works are given in centimetres (cm), height preceding width followed by depth.

Care has been taken to ensure the colour reproductions match as closely as possible the digital files of the original works.

Typeset in Veneer, Corki and Flama.
Image colour adjustment by ColourChiefs and printing by Cornerstone Press. Printed on Strathmore Premium Wove and HannoArt Silk from KW Doggett Fine Paper.

Cover:
Kitchen blues 2009
Gouache
9.8 x 14.8cm
Collection: Michael and Kylie Rayner, Brisbane

Page 2:
The artist in her studio c.1983
Madonna Staunton archive

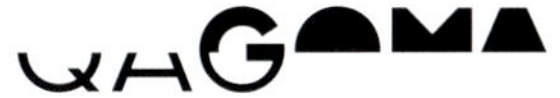

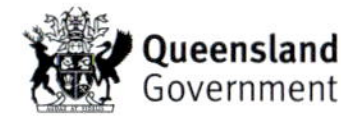

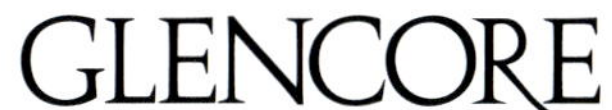